THE RED BARON

THE RED BARON

MANFRED FREIHERR VON RICHTHOFEN
Rittmeister, Imperial German Air Service

Translated by
PETER KILDUFF

BARNES
&NOBLE
BOOKS
NEW YORK

This edition published by Barnes & Noble, Inc.,
by arrangement with Stanley M. Ulanoff.

1995 Barnes & Noble Books

ISBN 1-56619-839-9

Printed and bound in the United States of America

M 9 8 7 6 5 4 3 2 1

ACKNOWLEDGMENTS

I am most grateful to fellow *Cross & Cockade* members Peter Kilduff, for his excellent translation from Von Richthofen's original German copy of *Der Rote Kampfflieger;* and Joe Phelan, for his three-view drawings of World War I aircraft and the handsome dust covers he designed for this Air Combat Classics series.

I must also acknowledge with much appreciation the support that Doubleday & Company, and particularly Harold Kuebler, have given to this series. Their confidence in bringing back these exciting, rare collectors' items that were originally published at the close of the First World War and have been long out of print, has been more than justified by the eager response of many thousands of readers.

My appreciation goes as well to the United States Air Force and National Archives for most of the very excellent photos used to illustrate this volume, to Major Eric R. Lifvergren for the personal photos he provided, to Hanns-Gerd Rabe of Germany for his help with the research, to Revell, Inc., for the use of their splendid three-view aircraft drawings, to Twentieth Century-Fox for their photo of the "Blue Max" medal from the film of the same name, and to Susan Bernstein and Joan Farley for their typing. Thanks, too, to my friend Clyde Risley for the pen-and-ink sketch of the Red Baron he drew especially for this volume.

Stanley M. Ulanoff, Editor

CONTENTS

LIST OF PHOTOGRAPHS

1. Rittmeister Manfred Freiherr von Richthofen
2. The Baron and his famous Jagdstaffel 11
3. Von Richthofen suiting up to go aloft in his Albatros
4. Von Richthofen making last-minute adjustments to his flight suit prior to taking off in his Albatros D V from a naval air station
5. Von Richthofen speaking with a fellow officer in front of his famous all-red Fokker triplane
6. Captain A. Roy Brown, the Canadian flier credited with shooting down the Red Baron
7. Oberleutnant Max Immelmann
8. Werner Voss and his motorcycle
9. Oberleutnant Ernst Udet
10. Ernst Udet, Bruno Loerzer, and their friend Siegmund Abel
11. Lothar von Richthofen, younger brother of the Red Baron, and his Fokker D VII
12. Hermann Göring in the cockpit of his Fokker triplane
13. "Fat Hermann" during later, inglorious Nazi times
14. General Erich Ludendorff, Chief of Staff to Field Marshal Paul von Hindenburg
15. Field Marshal Paul von Hindenburg, victor over the Russians at Tannenberg, Supreme Commander of the Central Powers forces, and later President of the German Republic
16. Kaiser Wilhelm

LIST OF DRAWINGS

INTRODUCTION TO NEW EDITION

Over fifty years after Rittmeister (Captain) Manfred Freiherr (Baron) von Richthofen blazed his deeds across the skies over the scarred battlefields of World War I to become a legend in his own time, he has come to life again. He lives on in a comic strip as the adversary of an air-minded dog named "Snoopy." Today, because of that cartoon character, the "Red Baron" has become a household name in the United States. But there are few who really know who he was or, for that matter, whether or not he ever even existed.

This book, which he wrote as a sort of personal diary during the war, was originally published in Berlin in 1918. Attesting to his reputation as a worthy and formidable opponent, two British publishers immediately brought out editions translated into English.

This edition of *The Red Baron* is a brand-new translation, the first to be published by an American firm. It is the first English translation of the 1933 edition, into which had been incorporated Von Richthofen's First World War letters. This volume also contains an account by his younger brother, Lothar, who was a leading German ace in his own right. Lothar was a member of the Baron's *staffel* and often flew as his brother's wingmate. In addition, the reader will find an introductory piece by Von Richthofen's youngest brother, Bolko, as well as Bolko's description of the return of Manfred's body from France to the "fatherland." Here too is an account purported to be by Captain A. Roy Brown describing the events of Von Richthofen's last fight.

Since much has been written here by Hermann Göring, and

brothers Lothar and Bolko, of the Red Baron's exploits, I will not go into further detail. However, the following observations may be of interest to the reader.

An analysis of the Red Baron's confirmed victories indicates that he flew principally against the British Royal Flying Corps (RFC), Royal Air Force (RAF), and Royal Naval Air Service (RNAS). Of his 80 victories, 79 were scored against British-manned aircraft, accounting for the death, wounding, or capture of 126 British fliers. (The greater number of personnel than planes is accounted for by the fact that more than half, 46, of the aircraft brought down by Von Richthofen were two-seaters.)

Only one lone Belgian, flying a Spad VII, interrupted the Red Baron's string of coups against his British antagonists. No Frenchmen fell before his guns, nor did any Americans. Although Von Richthofen did claim a Farman piloted by a Frenchman in September 1915, and a French-flown Nieuport 11 in April of 1916, these aircraft were not officially credited to him.

The explanation for Von Richthofen's not having done battle against Americans is simple. The first official patrol flown by the AEF took place on 14 April 1918, precisely one week before the Baron's death. However, he might have met Americans flying with the British or the *Lafayette Escadrille*. It is strange that he rarely engaged the French in combat, nor did he claim any Spad XIIIs, which replaced the Spad VIIs in the French fighter squadrons in the summer and fall of 1917. No Nieuport 28s fell victim to his twin Spandaus either, since that aircraft saw action principally with the AEF.

The legend of the Red Baron lived on in defeated Germany in the twenties and thirties, and in World War II an elite *Luftwaffe* flying unit was named after him. Members of his original *staffel* and *geschwader* who also served in the Second World War, such as Udet and Göring, wore a special red band attesting to the fact around the lower part of the right sleeve.

In preparing this new translation the editors have taken the liberty of attempting to smooth out the strange inconsistencies in language and in the chronological sequence of events as printed in both the 1918 and 1933 editions. One can only assume that this would have been done by the Rittmeister himself had he survived the war. In any event, we trust the reader will find this edition more readable and less confusing, than the previous versions.

STANLEY M. ULANOFF
Editor

MY LIFE IN THE WAR

BY

Manfred Freiherr von Richthofen

Cadet Life
(1903–9 Wahlstatt, 1909–11 Lichterfelde)

I entered the Cadet Corps as a boy of eleven. I was not particularly eager to become a cadet, but my father wished it, and I was not consulted.

I found it difficult to bear the strict discipline and order. I did not care very much for the instruction I received, and I was never good at learning things. I did just enough work to pass. In my opinion, it would have been wrong to do more than was necessary, so I worked as little as possible. As a result, my teachers did not have high regard for me. On the other hand, I was very fond of sports, particularly gymnastics, soccer and the like. I could do all manner of stunts on the horizontal bar, and I soon received prizes from the commandant of the school.

I had a great liking for risky tricks. One fine day my friend Frankenberg and I climbed the well-known steeple of Wahlstatt by going up the lightning rod. I tied my handkerchief to the top of the steeple. I remember vividly how difficult it had been to negotiate the gutters along the way. Ten years later I visited my youngest brother, Bolko, at Wahlstatt, and I saw my handkerchief still tied high in the air.

My friend Frankenberg was the first victim of the war, as far as I know.

I liked the school at Lichterfelde much better. I did not feel so isolated from the world, and I began to live more like a human being. My happiest memories of Lichterfelde are those of the great sporting events when my opponent was Prince Friedrich Karl of Prussia.[1] The Prince won many first prizes and other awards beyond mine, as I had not trained as carefully as he had.

Entrance Into the Army

Naturally, I could scarcely wait, during Easter of 1911, to go into the Army. Therefore, after my officer's examination I went right to Uhlan Regiment 1, "Kaiser Alexander III." I had chosen this regiment because it was in my beloved Silesia, and I had some friends and relatives there as well. Service with my regiment was very enjoyable. It is the most wonderful thing for a young soldier to be a cavalryman.

I can say little about my military school time. It was very similar to the Cadet Corps, and because of that, it is not too pleasant a memory.

A funny thing happened about this time, though. One of my military-school instructors had bought a nice fat mare named Biffy. Her one defect was that she was about fifteen years old. She had somewhat fat legs, but was otherwise an excellent jumper. I rode her often.

[1] Prince Friedrich Karl of Prussia, son of Kaiser Wilhelm II, also served in the German Air Force, first as an observer and then as a fighter pilot. He was flying with *Jagdstaffel* 2 (a unit Manfred von Richthofen served with early in his career) when he was shot down on March 22, 1917. Prince Friedrich Karl subsequently died from the wounds received in that engagement.

About a year later a cavalry captain in the regiment who was a sports enthusiast told me that he had bought a rather clumsy eight-year-old jumping horse. We were all curious about the "clumsy jumper" that bore the name Biffy. I had no further thoughts of the mare of my military-school teacher, but the day the wonderful animal arrived I was amazed to find that good old Biffy had turned up as an eight-year-old in the captain's stable. She had changed masters several times and risen in value. My academy teacher had bought her for 1500 Marks, and the captain acquired her a year later as an eight-year-old for 3500 Marks. She won more jumping competitions, but she changed masters again. She was killed at the beginning of the war.

I Become an Officer

(AUTUMN 1912)

Finally I received my epaulettes and was so proud to be addressed as *"Herr Leutnant."*

My father bought me a beautiful mare named Santuzza. She was the most wonderful animal, virtually indestructible but gentle as a lamb. I discovered she had a great talent for jumping, so I decided to make a jumping horse out of her.

I found great support and much understanding in a comrade named Von Wendel, who had won many beautiful prizes with his charger Fandango.

We both trained for a jumping competition and distance race to be held in Breslau. Fandango trained splendidly and, through great effort, Santuzza also did well. I had hoped to win some event with her. On the day before she was to be loaded on the train I could not resist taking her over the hurdles in our training area once more. In so doing we slipped. Santuzza bruised her shoulder and I cracked my collarbone.

From her speed in training I expected a fine performance from Santuzza, and, despite Fandango's great record, I was very disappointed when Von Wendel's thoroughbred defeated her.

Another time I had the good fortune to ride a very beautiful chestnut bay horse, Felix, at the Olympiad in Breslau. In the distance race my horse, a gelding, was hale and hearty, even in the second third of the course, and so I had hopes of success. Then came the last obstacle. I saw from a distance that it must be something special, as a crowd of people had gathered there. I thought to myself, "Cheer up, there's worse to come!" and came winding up over the embankment, on top of which was a brace. People waved to me not to ride so fast, but I saw and heard nothing. My horse took the brace right off and, to my great astonishment, went into the Weistritz River on the other side. Before I could act, the animal had jumped into the river, and mount and rider disappeared. Naturally, we went "head over heels." Felix came out on one side, and Manfred on the other. At the weigh-in at the end of the race, people were amazed that I had not lost the usual two pounds, but, rather, was ten pounds heavier. Thank God, no one saw that I was soaking wet.

I also owned a very good charger, and this unfortunate animal had to do everything: running, distance racing, jumping competition, parade marching. In short, there was no practice in which this fine animal had not been trained. Her name was Flower, and I achieved some very fine wins on her. My last victory was the Kaiser Prize Race of 1913. I was the only one to take the whole circuit without a mistake. Something happened to me that could not be easily duplicated. I galloped over the heather, and then, suddenly, landed on my head. The horse had stepped into a rabbit hole and, in the fall, I had broken my collarbone. I remounted and rode another seventy kilometers with the injury, but finished in good time without making a mistake.

In all the newspapers at this time there was nothing but inflated stories about the war. But for some months we had become accustomed to such "war talk." We had packed up our service kits so often that it became boring and we no longer believed in the war. We who were on the border, the "eyes of the Army," as the commander of our cavalry patrol had said, believed least in the possibility of war.

On the evening before the stepped-up war preparation we sat with men from a detached squadron, ten kilometers from the border, in our officers' mess, gambling a little. We were very cheerful. As I said, no one thought of war.

I admit, though, that Wedel's mother had startled us a few days before. She had come from Pomerania in order to see her son once more before the war began. She found us in the best spirits and must have realized that we did not think much of all the war talk. Reassured, she could not help but invite us to a proper breakfast. We were all very merry when, suddenly, the door opened and Count Kospoth, the district magistrate of Ols, stood on the threshold. The Count looked startled.

We greeted this old friend warmly. He explained to us that he had come to the border personally to convince himself that the rumors of the impending World War were true. He took it, quite correctly, that the best information could be obtained at the border. Now he was more than a little surprised to see this peaceful picture. We learned from him that all of the bridges in Silesia were being guarded and the fortification of some important places was being considered.

We quickly convinced him that war was out of the question and continued our celebration.

The next day we went to war.

Outbreak of War
(A LETTER)

Ostrowo, 2 August 1914

These, in great haste, may be my last lines. I greet you all sincerely. If we should not see each other again, you have my most sincere thanks for all you have done. I have no debts; indeed, I am even taking eight hundred Marks with me.

I embrace each of you.

Your grateful and obedient son and brother.

Manfred

Crossing the Border

The word "war" was certainly familiar to us border cavalry-men. Each of us knew to the smallest detail what to do and what to leave undone. But no one had any idea what would happen next. Every soldier on active duty was eager to show his personal worth and knowledge.

The most interesting tasks were assigned to the young cavalry lieutenants: reconnoitering the enemy's positions, and destroying important installations, jobs that required a real man to do.

With orders in my pocket, the importance of which had been impressed on me by a year of study, I rode at the head of my patrol at midnight against the enemy for the first time.

The Russian border was formed by a river, and I expected to be fired upon there for the first time. I was greatly surprised that we were able to pass over the bridge without incident. Still without further incident the next morning, we reached the church tower of the village of Kieltze, which was known to us from our border rides.

The day passed without our seeing a single one of the enemy or, rather, without being seen by him. My first thought was to place the local Orthodox priest under lock and key. So we fetched the startled man from his house. Next thing, I locked him in the belfry of the church tower, took away the ladder, and left him to sit there. I assured him that if the slightest hostile behavior was noticed among the population, he would immediately be doomed to death. A sentinel was placed on the lookout in the tower and observed the neighborhood.

I had to send daily reports back to headquarters by dispatch riders. My small troop of men were gradually being reduced by this dispatch riding, and it was apparent that I would have to make the last trip myself.

Everything remained quiet up until the fifth night. At that time the sentinel from the church tower—near where I had put my horse—came to me and cried out: "The Cossacks are here!" It was pitch-black, a bit rainy, no stars. You could not see a hand in front of you.

We led the horses through a place in the church wall that had already been opened as a precautionary measure and moved into the open field. After fifteen meters through the darkness, we were in complete safety. I myself went with the sentinel, carbine in hand, to the designated place where the Cossacks would have been.

I glided along the churchyard wall and came to the street. A strange feeling came over me, for the village road was swarming with Cossacks. I peered over the wall, behind which these fellows had put their horses. Most of the men had lanterns and carried on loudly and without caution. I estimated that there were twenty to thirty of them. One had dismounted and gone to the Orthodox priest, whom I had released the day before.

Of course, "We are betrayed!" flashed through my brain. Therefore, we had to be doubly alert. I could not chance a battle, for I now had no more than two carbines at my disposal. Therefore, I played "cops and robbers."

After some hours of rest, our visitors rode away again.

The next day I thought we had better change our quarters. On the seventh day I was again back in my garrison, and everyone stared at me as if I were a ghost, not only because of my unshaven face, but much more because of the widespread rumor that Wedel and I had fallen when the Cossacks took Kalisch. The time and place and related circumstances had been told so exactly that the rumor spread widely throughout all Silesia. My mother had already received condolence visits.

All that was lacking was the obituary notice in the newspaper.

About this time a veterinarian was ordered to requisition ten horses for the Uhlans from a farm about three kilometers from the main road. He came back quite excited and reported the following:

"I was riding over a stubble field, in which there were scarecrows, when suddenly from a distance I saw enemy infantry. Quickly I decided to draw my saber and call to my Uhlans: 'Lances! Attack! Forward! Forward! Hurrah!' It was great fun for the men to begin this wild chase over the stubble. But, alas, the enemy infantry turned out to be a flock of deer that my shortsightedness had taken to be soldiers by mistake."

That fine gentleman had to suffer for a long time because of this "gallant" attack.

(A LETTER)

Schelmce, southwest of Kalisch, 5 August 1914
How do you like what is happening in these stirring times? In Schweidnitz you are certainly most secure. I am already

in the third night of patrol in Russia. There are no German troops ahead of me; therefore I am the farthest advanced. One becomes crude with lightning speed. I find it quite natural that I have not been able to remove my clothes in four days or wash properly since the declaration of war. My six men and I sleep very little—and then, naturally, only under the open sky. The nights are beautifully warm, but today, when it rained, it was hardly amusing. There is little to eat; only with threats of violence can one get anything. None of my men is wounded. When you get this letter I will perhaps already be at the French border. The cannons are thundering in the vicinity of Kalisch, I must see what's going on. I send you all sincere greetings from nearby Russia.

Your Manfred

To France

The garrison packed and we were ready to go. Where to? We had no idea if it would be west, east, south or north. There were many rumors, but most just faded away. But this time we had the right idea: westward.

Four of us were assigned to a second-class train compartment. We had to take provisions for a long railroad journey. Naturally, we did not lack for something to drink. On the first day we discovered that a second-class compartment was much too narrow for four warlike men, and so we resolved to spread ourselves out. I converted half of a baggage car into a living room and bedroom, for greater comfort. I had air, light, etc. I procured straw at one station stop and covered it with a tent cloth. I slept as well in my sleeping car as I had in the family bed in Ostrowa. The journey lasted for a day and a night, through all of Silesia and Saxony, always moving toward the west. It seemed we were going in the direction of

Metz; the train conductor himself did not know where we were going. At every station, even at those where we did not stop, we were greeted by a sea of people, overwhelming us with cheers and flowers. The Uhlans were especially admired. The train that passed the station before us had probably reported that our regiment had already met the enemy—and we were in the first eight days of the war. In addition, my regiment was mentioned in the first army communiqué. Uhlan Regiment 1 and Infantry Regiment 155 had taken Kalisch. We were, therefore, celebrated heroes and even felt as such. Wedel had found a Cossack sword and made a great impression showing it to wide-eyed girls. Finally we disembarked at Busendorf, near Diedenhofen.

Shortly before the train arrived we were stopped in a long tunnel. I must say that it is bad enough to be stopped in a tunnel in peacetime, but even more so in wartime. This time some high-spirited fellow wanted to have some fun and fired a shot. It didn't take long for disorderly shooting to start everywhere in the tunnel. The origin of the shooting, however, was never determined.

It was so hot at Busendorf that our horses threatened to give in. During the next few days we marched ever northward in the direction of Luxembourg. Meanwhile, I discovered that my brother had ridden along the same route about a week before with a cavalry division. I picked up his trail, but I didn't see him again until a year later.

In Luxembourg no one knew where this little state stood politically in relation to us. I only knew that when I saw a Luxembourg policeman in the distance, my patrol surrounded him and took him prisoner. He protested to me that if we did not let him go, he would complain to the German Kaiser. I saw reason in that, so I let this prominent person go. We continued on through Luxembourg and Esch and, finally, approached the first fortified cities of Belgium.

During the advance our infantry, as well as our whole division, maneuvered just as in peacetime. The men were quite excited. But such an advancing maneuver was good for everyone. Under any circumstances the men would have upset all traces of order. Right and left, on every street, in front of us and behind us marched troops of different army corps. One felt that everything was in disorderly confusion, but, suddenly, from out of this motley crowd, a splendidly functional force evolved.

At the time I hadn't the slightest idea what our fliers did. I considered every flier an enormous fraud. I could not tell if he were friend or foe. I had no idea that German machines bore crosses and the enemy's had cockades. As a result, every flier came under our fire. Even today the old pilots tell how painful it was to be fired at by friend and foe alike.

We marched and marched, with patrols far ahead, until one fine day we arrived at Arlon. I had a funny feeling as I crossed a border for the second time. Obscure reports of *franc-tireurs*[2] had already reached us.

One time I was ordered to liaison duties with my cavalry division. On that day I rode no less than one hundred and ten kilometers with my whole patrol. Not a horse failed us— a splendid achievement of our animals. In Arlon I climbed the church tower, using the skills of boyhood; naturally, I saw nothing, as the evil enemy was still far away.

At the time we were relatively harmless. Thus, for example, I had my patrol stay behind while I rode alone on a bicycle through the city to the church tower. When I came down from the tower I found myself in the midst of a group of grumbling, muttering, hostile-looking [Belgian] youths. My bicycle, naturally, had been made off with and I had to go by foot for half an hour. But this amused me. I would like to have gotten

---

2 *Franc-tireurs* were sharpshooters, trained to lie in wait for passing enemy troops.

in a little scuffle. I felt quite secure with my service pistol in
my hand.

The inhabitants, as I later learned, had rebelled against our
cavalry a few days earlier and, later, even against our hospital,
so it had been necessary to line a number of them up against
the wall.

In the afternoon I reached my destination and learned that,
three days earlier, my only cousin Richthofen had fallen in
the region of Arlon. I stayed the rest of the day with a cavalry
division, accompanied it on a false alarm, and late that night
came back to my own regiment.

We experienced and saw more than the others; we even had
more contact with the enemy. Having seen the imprint of the
war, we were envied by the men in the other branches of
service. It was quite wonderful; indeed, the most enjoyable
time in the whole war. I would like very much to participate in
the beginning of a war again.

(A LETTER)

In the vicinity of Diedenhofen
I will briefly describe for you what I have experienced here
on the Western Front. Before the advance of the army ended,
it was somewhat boring. We disembarked northeast of Diedenhofen and marched through Luxembourg and crossed
the Belgian border near Arlon. In Etalle, about twenty kilometers west of Arlon, I was ordered on 21 August to recon-
noiter south in the direction of Meix-devant-Virton. As I came
to the edge of the forest south of Etalle, I spotted a troop of
French dragoons. I only had fifteen men with me. After about
a half hour the enemy troop disappeared and I led my men
forward to determine where the French had gone. We found
ourselves right at the exit of the forest, in the vicinity of Meix-
devant-Virton. On the right was a wall of rock, on the left a

stream, and about fifty meters behind was a broad meadow—then the forest's edge. Suddenly my horse stopped short, but I galloped out to see what was going on.

Just as I put the field glasses to my eye, a volley of fire cracked from the edge of the forest about fifty meters away. There were about two hundred to two hundred and fifty French riflemen over there. We couldn't move to the left or forward because the enemy was there, and to the right was the wall of rock; therefore, we had to go back. Yes, but it wasn't so simple. The way was quite narrow and it led right by the enemy-fortified forest's edge. To take cover was also useless; therefore I had to go back. I was the last one. In spite of my orders, all the others had bunched together and offered the Frenchmen a good target. Perhaps that was the reason why I escaped. I brought only four men back. This baptism of fire was not as much fun as I thought. That evening some of the others came back, although they had to come by foot, as their horses were dead.

It was really a miracle that nothing happened to me or my horse.

The same night I was sent to Virton but did not get there as that town was taken by the enemy.

During the night Division Commander Von Below decided to attack the enemy at Virton and appeared at the head of his Uhlan Regiment 1 at the exit of the forest.

The fog was so thick, one could not see more than thirty paces ahead.

One regiment after another, just as if on maneuvers, was deployed on the narrow way into the forest. Prince Oscar stood on a pile of rocks and urged his regiment, the 7th Grenadiers, onward, looking each grenadier in the eye. A splendid moment before the battle. Thus began the battle of Virton, where the 9th Division fought against an enemy six times its own number, and where, after two days, was brilliantly victorious.

In this battle Prince Oscar fought at the head of his regiment and remained unscathed. I spoke with him right after the battle, as he was presented with the Iron Cross.

How I Heard the Whistling of Bullets the First Time on Patrol (21–22 August 1914)

I had been ordered to determine the strength of the enemy force in a great forest near Virton. I rode out with fifteen Uhlans, and it was clear to me that the first encounter with the enemy would be that day. My orders were not easy, for in such a forest many terrible things could be hidden.

I came over a hill. A few hundred paces before me lay a vast forest of several thousand acres. It was a beautiful August morning. The forest lay so peaceful and quiet that one could hardly think about the war.

We approached the point of entrance to the forest. We could see nothing suspicious through field glasses, so we were forced to ride on to see if we would be fired upon. The men in front disappeared along the forest lane. I was next, and near me rode one of my good Uhlans. A lone forester's cottage stood at the entrance to the forest. We rode by it. Suddenly a shot came from a window in the house. And then another shot. From the report I could tell it was not from a carbine, but from a musket. There was disorder in my patrol. I surmised this to be an ambush by *franc-tireurs*. From horseback it looked like the work of one person. I had the house surrounded to prevent escape, and then entered. In one rather dark room I saw four or five hostile-looking boys. Their muskets, of course, were not to be seen. My anger was high at the moment, but I had never killed anyone in my life, and so I must say the moment was extremely unpleasant. But I had to crack down on the *franc-tireurs*. One of them had fired a load of buckshot into the belly of one of the horses and had wounded one of my Uhlans in the hand as well.

In my wretched French I shouted at the bandits, demanding they turn over the guilty one, or everyone in the house would be shot. They saw that I meant business and would not hesitate to act on my words. What really happened after that I don't know to this day. In any case, the *franc-tireurs* dashed out the back door and disappeared into the woods. I fired after them, but did not hit them. I immediately ordered the whole house ransacked, but nothing was found, the place was empty. We found only the musket piece standing by the window and had to avenge ourselves in a different way. In five minutes the house was in flames.

After this interlude we rode on.

I recognized from the fresh horse tracks that a strong force of enemy cavalry had marched directly ahead of us. I stopped my patrol and gave the men a few words of encouragement. I felt that I could depend absolutely on every one of them, and I knew that in the next few minutes each would have to depend on the other. Naturally, no one thought of anything else than attacking. It is in the blood of every German to rush out to meet the enemy, especially enemy cavalry. I already saw myself at the head of my little band, cutting an enemy squadron to pieces, and quite drunk with joyful expectation. The eyes of my Uhlans sparkled. So we went along the trail at a rapid trot. After an hour's ride through the beautiful glen the forest became somewhat thinner and we neared the exit. It was clear that we would meet the enemy. Therefore, we had to move with caution! All were looking forward to the attack. To the right of our narrow path was a rock wall many meters high. To our left was a narrow mountain stream, then a meadow fifty meters wide, surrounded by barbed wire. Suddenly the patter of the horses stopped and disappeared over a bridge and into the bushes. My leading men were forced to stop because the exit from the forest was blocked by a barricade.

It was immediately clear that I had fallen into a trap. I suddenly saw movement in the bushes behind the meadow to my left; then I could make out the dismounted enemy cavalry. I estimated them to be one hundred rifles strong. Nothing could be done here. Straight ahead the way was blocked by the barricade; to the right was the rock wall; to the left my original plan of attack was hindered by the wire surrounding the meadow. There was no time to dismount and attack the enemy with carbines. There was nothing left to do but go back. I could depend on my good Uhlans to do everything but retreat before the enemy. That ruined our fun.

A second later we heard the first shot, followed by intensive rifle fire from the woods. The distance was about fifty to a hundred meters. The men were instructed to join me when I lifted my hand. Now I knew we had to go back, so I lifted my arm and motioned to them. It is possible they misunderstood my gesture. The patrol which I left behind believed me to be in danger and came in a wild charge to help me get away. We were on a narrow path, so it is easy to imagine the resulting confusion. The horses of the men riding ahead rushed away in panic, because the noise of every shot was increased fourteenfold by the narrowness of the path. They cleared the barricade in one jump and I never saw them again. Certainly they were captured. I myself spun around and gave my good horse, Antithesis, the spurs for the first time in his life. It was very difficult to make myself understood to the Uhlans riding toward me, to tell them not to go forward. Turn around and out! My orderly rode nearby. Suddenly his horse was hit and fell. I jumped over them while horses were rolling all around me. It was wild disorder. The last I saw of my orderly, he lay under his horse, apparently not wounded but held down by the weight of the animal. The enemy had surprised us splendidly. He had probably observed us from the beginning and, as the Frenchmen do, intended to catch us unawares, which he successfully did in this case.

Two days later I was delighted when my orderly appeared before me wearing only one boot, as he had left the other under his horse. He told me how he had escaped: At least two squadrons of French dragoons had come out of the forest to plunder the fallen horses and brave Uhlans. As he was not wounded, he had jumped up, climbed the rock wall, and fell down in exhaustion among the bushes fifty meters away. About two hours later, after the enemy had set up the ambush again, he continued his flight. A few days later he joined me. He could tell little of the fate of our other comrades.

Patrol Ride with Loen

While the battle of Virton was going on, my comrade Loen and I were ordered once again to determine where the enemy was. We rode on patrol the whole day and finally found the enemy in the evening. The big question now was: Will we ride through the night in order to get back to our troops, or shall we rest and save our strength for the next day? That is the beautiful part about being a cavalryman on patrol: He is given a completely free hand.

We decided to stay the night near the enemy and ride back the next morning. Our notes of the enemy showed he was pulling back, and we followed him. Consequently, we were able to spend the night with some security.

Now, far from the enemy there was a wonderful monastery with large stables, so that Loen and I as well as our whole patrol could be quartered there. The enemy was so close he could have shot us through the window. But the monks were very friendly. They gave us as much to eat and drink as we wanted, which we consumed with delight. The saddles were taken off the horses and they were quite happy when, for the first time in three days and three nights, a dead weight of eighty kilos was removed from their backs. In other words, we settled down as if we were on maneuvers and in the house of a fine host for the evening. It should be noted at the same time that three days later we hanged several of our hosts from lampposts because they could not resist the urge to take part in the war. But that evening they were extremely friendly. We put on our nightshirts and got into bed, posted a sentry, and let the good Lord look after us.

That night the door suddenly flew open and the voice of the sentry resounded: *"Herr Leutnant,* the French are here." I was really too sleepy to give an answer. Loen was similarly indisposed, but he made the most intelligent reply: "How many are there?" The sentry answered excitedly: "We have already shot two of them dead; we cannot say how many there are, it is pitch-black outside." I heard Loen, still half-asleep, answer: "If any more come, wake me up." Half a minute later we were snoring again.

The next morning the sun was high in the sky when we woke up from our refreshing sleep. After a good breakfast we continued the journey.

During the night the French had actually marched past our castle and our sentries had indeed fired on them. Since it had been pitch-black outside, no further battle could take place.

Soon we passed through a lovely valley. We rode over the old battlefield of our division and were surprised that, instead of seeing our men, we saw French medical orderlies there. French soldiers were also to be seen here and there. They had even dumber expressions than we had. No one thought of shooting. We quickly made ourselves scarce, for it occurred to us that, instead of going forward, our forces had concentrated in the rear. Luckily, the opponent was also pulling out; otherwise we would have been imprisoned somewhere.

We came through the village of Robelmont, which we had seen our infantry occupy on the previous day. We encountered one inhabitant and inquired of the fate of our soldiers. He was very happy and assured me the Germans were *"partis."*

We came around a corner and were witnesses to the following comic scene. Before us was a swarm of men in red trousers—I estimated fifty to a hundred—struggling hard to dash their weapons to pieces. Nearby stood six grenadiers who, it was later proven, had taken their brothers prisoner. We helped them to transport the Frenchmen and learned from the six grenadiers that we would set out on a rearward movement that night.

In late afternoon I reached my regiment and was quite satisfied with the outcome of the last twenty-four hours.

(A LETTER)

Behind Metz, before Paris, near Verdun,
September 1914

Best of thanks for both of your last cards of the twenty-first and twenty-fourth. The mail comes quite irregularly. I received the card of the twenty-fourth a week before the other. I also received a package of sweets. Many thanks! For about a week a cavalry division has been near Paris. I almost believe that Lothar has the good fortune to be with that division. He has certainly experienced more than I have sitting here near Verdun. The army of the Crown Prince will surround Verdun from here northwards, until it surrenders. Verdun will not be stormed, only sealed off. The fortifications are too strong and would require excessive amounts of munitions and lives to take by storm. The occupation of Verdun would not benefit us accordingly. It is only too bad that we of Uhlan 1 are tied up here and the war will most likely end here. The battle for Verdun is very hard and claims an immense number of lives daily. Yesterday eight officers from the 7th Grenadiers fell during an attack.

(A LETTER)

Before Verdun, 24 September 1914

I can announce joyful tidings to you. Yesterday I received the Iron Cross.

How is everything with Lemberg? I will give you some advice: If the Russians come, bury everything you want to see again deep in the garden or somewhere else. What you leave out, you will never see again.

You wonder that I save so much money, but after the war I will have to buy everything new for myself. What I have taken with me is finished—lost, burned, mangled by shells, etc., including my saddle and harness. If I should live through this war, I will have more luck than sense.

Boredom Before Verdun

For such a restless soul am I, my activity before Verdun was marked by boredom. In the beginning I was in the trenches in a place where nothing happened; then I became an assistant adjutant and believed I would experience more. But I was sadly mistaken. I was degraded from being one of the fighting men to being a "paper shuffler." I was not really that low, but the farthest I was allowed to go was fifteen hundred meters behind the front lines. There I sat for weeks on end underground in a bomb-proof, heated dugout. Back and forth I went taking things here and there. That was a great physical strain. For I went uphill, downhill, crisscross, through an unending number of trenches and mudholes until I finally came to where the firing was going on. After a short visit with the fighting men, it seemed to be a very stupid thing for me to be doing.

At that time they began digging underground. It was not yet clear to us what it meant to dig tunnels and trenches. Of course we knew the names from fortification lessons in the War Academy, but it was for engineers, with whom other mortals had no business. But up here near Combres everyone dug busily. Every man had a spade and a pick and gave unending effort to dig as deeply as possible into the ground. It was quite funny that in many places the French were only five paces ahead of us. We heard them talking, and saw them smoking cigarettes. Now and then they threw us a piece of paper. We conversed with them, but we still sought to annoy them in every way possible—especially with hand grenades.

Five hundred meters in front of us and five hundred meters behind the trenches the dense forest of Côte Lorraine had been cut down by the unending bullets and shells that whistled through the air. It was hard to believe that men could live up front. The troops up there, however, found it to be not quite as bad as in the base camp.

After a walk, usually in the early hours of the morning, the boring part of the day began for me, namely attending to the telephones.

On my free days I busied myself with my favorite pastime, hunting. The forest of La Chaussée offered me ample opportunity. During a leisurely ride I had noticed wild pigs and I was now busy trying to find out how I could shoot them at night. Beautiful moonlit nights with snow came to my aid. With the help of my orderly I built a shelter seat and waited at night. I spent many nights in trees and found in the morning I had become like an icicle. But I was rewarded. One sow was especially interesting. She swam across the lake every night, broke into a potato field at a certain place and then swam back again. Of course it made me especially want to get to know this animal better. So I took my place on the shore of the lake. As agreed upon, the old "aunt" appeared at midnight for her supper. I shot her as she swam in the lake, and she would have drowned if I had not at the last moment seized her by the leg.

Another time I was riding with my orderly along a narrow path when several wild pigs crossed in front of me. I immediately jumped down from my horse, grabbed my orderly's carbine, and ran several hundred paces ahead. Then came quite a fellow—in fact, a mighty boar. I had never seen a boar before, and I was amazed at how gigantic this fellow looked. Now he hangs as a trophy here in my room; he is a beautiful memory.

(A LETTER)

Before Verdun, 11 October 1914

The mail is just going out and I would like to send a greeting to you. In the last days I have experienced many things. I almost died, but once again I was lucky. I was on patrol and had just gotten down from my fine charger when a grenade fell and exploded on the saddle of my horse. Three other horses lay dead from this action. My saddle and everything that one really needs and what I had in the saddlebag were ripped into small pieces. A fragment ripped through my cloak but did not touch me. I just read a letter from Aunt Friedel; I had not opened her package yet, but instead, had put it in my saddlebag—it was crushed into a shapeless mass. Antithesis is still with me; he received a small fragment in the molars—nothing more.

(A LETTER)

Béchamps, 2 November 1914

We are now in and out of the trenches, like the infantry; two thousand meters in front of us are the French. It is no fun to lie quietly for the duration of twenty-four boring hours. Some shells come back and forth in singular exchange; that is all I have experienced in the last four weeks. It is too bad we are not employed in the major battle. For weeks the position before Verdun has not shifted fifty meters. We are camped in a burned-out village. Wedel and I live in a house in which you must hold your nose. We seldom if ever ride, as Antithesis is sick and my chestnut bay is dead. In other words: There is no movement at all. Eating does little good: Nothing agrees with me—even though I am fat as a barrel. If I should ride again, I will need to exercise until I get back to my normal weight again. I would like very much to have gotten the Iron Cross, First Class, but there is no opportunity here. I must, then, go to Verdun dressed as a Frenchman and blow up a gun turret.

(A LETTER)

Côtes, 15 January 1915

Through a short announcement I have already let you know that I am the Assistant Adjutant of the 18th Infantry Brigade. Here one experiences somewhat more than with our regiment at Béchamps. In mobile warfare it is the other way around. So I am quite satisfied with my post. In the last days there was considerable activity before Côtes. On the night of the twenty-seventh to the twenty-eighth, we of Grenadier Regiment 7 took a trench from the French. On the night of the twenty-ninth to the thirtieth, the French tried to recover it but were splendidly crushed. Thank God the casualties were light. Every fellow here in the trenches is a hero, and the poet rightly said: "There is not so much iron as you heroes who are out there." Every single one deserves the Iron Cross; everyone who sees our brave men fighting must say that. Take care and give my best to Papa, Ilse and "Germany's future," Bolko.

Finally

After I had endured some months of this activity, one fine day there was some action involving our troops. We were supposed to take part in a minor offensive on our Front. I was extremely pleased because now I would have some work to do! But then came disappointment. I was given another job to do, and that was the last straw. I wrote a letter to my commanding general in which it was later falsely reported I had said: "My dear Excellency, I did not go to war to gather cheese and eggs, but for another purpose." At first people took offense at my request, but then it was granted, and so at the end of May 1915, I joined the Flying Service.[3] My greatest wish was fulfilled.

At seven o'clock the next morning I was to fly for the first time as an observer. Naturally, I was very excited, because I could not imagine what it would be like. Everyone I asked told me something different. The night before I had gone to bed earlier than usual to be fresh for the great moment next morning. We drove to the airfield and I sat in an airplane for the first time. The blast of wind from the propeller disturbed

[3] This is the first time Von Richthofen indicated an interest in becoming a flier, although the thought must have crossed his mind many times in those "boring hours" in and out of the trenches.

me greatly. It was impossible to make myself heard by the pilot. Everything flew away from me. If I took a piece of paper out, it disappeared. My flying helmet slipped off, my muffler loosened too much, and my jacket was not buttoned securely —in short, I was miserable. Before I knew what was happening, the pilot got the engine up to full speed and the machine began rolling, faster and faster. I hung on frantically. Then the shaking stopped and we were in the air. The ground slipped away beneath us.

I had been told where I was to fly, or, rather, where I was to direct my pilot to fly.[4] We flew straight ahead for a while, then my pilot made one turn after another, right and left, and I lost all sense of orientation to the airfield. I had no idea where I was! Very carefully I began to look over the side at the ground below. The people looked tiny and the houses looked like something out of a child's toybox, everything was so small and fine. In the background lay Cologne. The Cathedral looked like a plaything. It was a glorious feeling to sail over everything. Who could have touched me? No one! I didn't care where I was, and I was quite sad when the pilot said he thought we had better land.

I would rather have gone flying again. I have never been troubled with vertigo in the air. Moreover, the celebrated American Ferris wheel is repulsive to me; one feels insecure in it. But in an airplane one has an absolute feeling of security; one sits as peacefully as in an easy chair. It is out of the question for one to become giddy; one does not become giddy in an airplane. But it is a damned nervous sensation to whistle through the air, especially as the airplane suddenly dips, when the engine stops, and there is a tremendous silence. I held on frantically and, naturally, thought, "You're going to crash." But everything went along so naturally and

4 German observers were mainly officers and, hence, in command of the aircraft; pilots were N.C.O.s, acting as aerial "chauffeurs."

simply, even the landing when we touched down to earth again, that the feeling of fear was completely absent. I was very enthusiastic about it and could have stayed in the airplane all day. I counted the hours to the next flight.

(A LETTER)

Cologne, 6 June 1915

At last I have arrived here. There is a huge machine at *Flieger-Ersatz-Abteilung* [Air Replacement Station] 7 for us to train in. There are thirty of us, all to be trained as observers. For that reason, only the best will be selected and retained. It is under these extremely difficult and doubtful circumstances that I, fortunately, find myself one of these selectees.

As an Observer with Mackensen

On June 10, 1915, I reported to *Flieger-Ersatz-Abteilung* 6 at Grossenhain to complete my training. From there I was posted to *Feldfliegerabteilung* [Flying Section] 69 on the Eastern Front. Naturally, I was anxious to get to the Front. I was afraid I would get there too late and that the war might be over. I had had to spend three months to train as an observer; at the end of that time peace might have been concluded. Thus, it never occurred to me to train as a pilot. I felt that, due to my training as a cavalryman, I would do well as an observer. I was very happy when, after two weeks' flying experience, I was sent to the only place where there was still a chance to get in the active war: Russia.

General Von Mackensen was advancing gloriously. He had broken through the Russian position at Gorlice. I joined his army during the siege of Rawa Ruska. I spent a day at the aviation field headquarters, and then I was sent to *Feld-fliegerabteilung* 69. As a beginner I felt very foolish, but my pilot, *Oberleutnant* [First Lieutenant] Georg Zeumer, was very good. He is gone now.[5] In fact, of all the men in that unit, only I survive.

This was a wonderful time. Life in the air service was very much like life in the cavalry. Every day, morning and afternoon, I had to fly reconnaissance missions to gather valuable intelligence information.

With Holck in Russia

Through June, July and August of 1915 I remained with *Feldfliegerabteilung* 69, participating in Von Mackensen's great advance from Gorlice to Brest-Litovsk. I was a new observer with the unit, and I cared little about anything else. Reconnaissance had been my business in the cavalry, so I now served in my specialty and had great fun in the far-ranging reconnaissance flights we undertook almost every day.

It is most important for the observer to find a responsive pilot. So, when it was announced one fine day that Count Holck was coming to join us, I thought to myself: That is the man I need.

Holck appeared, not as one might expect, in a 60-hp Mercedes, or in a first-class sleeping car, but, rather, on foot. He had traveled for days by train until he finally arrived in the vicinity of Jaroslav. There he got off the train during a seemingly endless delay. He told his orderly to travel on with the luggage, while he went along on his own. He set out, and after

---

[5] *Oberleutnant* Georg Zeumer was later posted to *Jagdstaffel* 2 (which Von Richthofen had served in early in his career). Zeumer was shot down and killed June 17, 1917.

marching along for an hour he looked back, but no train followed. So he walked and walked without being overtaken by the train until, after fifty kilometers, he finally arrived in Rawa Ruska, his destination. Twenty-four hours later his orderly appeared with the luggage. Holck was a sportsman, so this was not unusual for him. His body was so well-conditioned that a fifty-kilometer march had little effect on him.

Erich Graf von Holck was not only a sportsman on the ground but in the air. Flying was a sport that gave him great pleasure as well. He was a pilot of rare talent, in a class by himself.

We flew many fine reconnaissances—who knows how far?—into Russia. I never had a greater feeling of security with so young a pilot; more than that, he was a great support in critical moments. When I looked into his determined face, I had even more courage than before.

My last flight with him nearly went awry. We had not really received definite orders to fly, which is indeed one of the nicest things about the air service. One is a free man and his own master in the air. But our airfield had been moved forward, and we did not really know which meadow was the right one. In order not to risk damaging our crate unnecessarily on landing, we flew toward Brest-Litovsk. The Russians were in full retreat, burning everything—a horribly beautiful sight. We intended to determine the strength of enemy columns, and, in so doing, came over the burning city of Wicznice. A gigantic pillar of smoke that reached up perhaps two thousand meters prevented us from completing our mission. In order to see better we had to do something, since we were only at fifteen hundred meters altitude. Holck thought about this for a moment. I asked him what he wanted to do and advised him to fly around it, which would be a detour of five minutes. But

Holck would have none of it. On the contrary: The greater
the danger, the more it attracted him. Therefore, he headed
right through it! It was fun to be with such a daring fellow.
But our carelessness soon cost us dearly, for scarcely had the
tail of the machine disappeared within the cloud when I noticed a swaying in the airplane. I could no longer look out,
the smoke stung my eyes, the air was noticeably hotter, and
beneath me I saw nothing but a sea of fire. Suddenly the airplane lost its lift and plunged downward. I grabbed a stay in
order to brace myself; otherwise, I would have been thrown
out. The first thing I did was look into Holck's face. I regained my courage, for his countenance was of iron confidence. The one thought that I had, however, was: It is stupid
to die a hero's death in such an unnecessary way.

Later I asked Holck what he had really thought at the moment. He said he had never been in such low spirits.

We plunged down to about five hundred meters above the
burning city. Whether it was through the skill of my pilot or
divine providence, or perhaps both—in any case, we suddenly
dropped out of the smoke cloud and our good Albatros once
again began to fly straight ahead as if nothing had happened.

We had now had enough of our assignment and we wanted
to get back to our own lines as soon as possible. We were, of
course, still over the Russian lines and only at five hundred
meters altitude. After about five minutes the voice of Holck
intoned behind me: "The engine is giving out."

I must add that Holck knew about as much about the engine
as he did about an old "hayburner," and I wasn't much better.
I only knew that if the engine quit we would have to land
among the Russians. Therefore, one danger came with the
other.

I was convinced by what I could see at our five-hundred-
meter altitude, that the Russians were marching briskly to-

ward us. However, I did not need to see them, because the Russkis shot diligently at us with their machine guns. It sounded like chestnuts popping in a fire.

Soon the engine stopped altogether; it had been hit. So we dropped lower and lower until we glided over a forest and landed at last in an abandoned artillery installation, which the evening before I had reported as a fortified Russian position.

I shared what I had seen with Holck. We jumped out of the old crate and attempted to reach the cover of the forest, where we could defend ourselves. I carried a pistol and six rounds; Holck had nothing.

When we reached the forest we stopped, and I saw through my field glasses that a soldier was running toward our airplane. I was horrified to see that he wore a cap and not a spiked helmet. That was a sure sign he was a Russian. But when the man came closer Holck shouted for joy, for he was a Prussian grenadier guard.

Our elite troops had once again stormed the position at daybreak and had come through the enemy battery.

I remember that on this occasion Holck lost his pet, a little dog. He took the little animal with him on every flight—he would lie in some fur down in the bottom of the fuselage. We still had him when we were in the forest. Shortly after that, when we had talked with the guardsman, German troops passed by. They were staff troops of the guards and Prince Eitel Friedrich and his adjutants and assistant adjutants. The Prince gave us horses, so once again we two cavalry fliers were mounted on "hay burning" motors. Unfortunately, the little dog was lost while we were riding. He must have followed other troops by mistake.

Late in the evening we arrived back at our airfield in an old cart. Our airplane was ruined.

Russia to Ostend

FROM THE TWO-SEATER TO THE LARGE BATTLE PLANE

After our venture in Russia gradually came to a halt, I was suddenly transferred on August 21, 1915, to *Brieftauben-Abteilung-Ostende* [Carrier Pigeon Unit, Ostend].[6] There I encountered my old friend Georg Zeumer. I was also fascinated by the name *"Grosskampfflugzeug"* [large battle plane] given to aircraft used by the B.A.

When I arrived in Ostend my friend Zeumer met me at the train station. Now I really had a nice time; it had little to do with the war, but it was essential to my apprenticeship as a combat flier. Zeumer and I flew a great deal, but we seldom had aerial combats, and we had no successes. The other life, however, was alluring. Our forces had expropriated a hotel on the beach at Ostend, where we bathed every afternoon. Unfortunately, the only visitors to the beach were soldiers. We sat on the terraces of Ostend, wrapped in gaily colored bathrobes, drinking coffee in the afternoon.

One time as we sat as usual along the beach, drinking coffee, there suddenly came the sound of a trumpet signaling the approach of an English naval squadron.

Naturally, we did not allow ourselves to be disturbed at the alarm and continued drinking our coffee. Someone called out, "There they are!" And we could actually see on the horizon, although not very distinctly, first some smokestacks and later some ships. Quickly we fetched field glasses and observed them. We saw quite an imposing number of ships. It was not clear what they intended to do, but we were soon to know

[6] A cover name to conceal the true activities of this unit

better. We went up to the roof to see more. Suddenly there
was a whistling in the air, followed by a tremendous explosion, and a shell hit a spot on the beach where we had been.
I never ran so fast to the bomb shelter as I did that moment.
The English naval squadron fired perhaps three or four times
and then concentrated on the main targets of Ostend—the
harbor and train station. Naturally, they hit nothing. But they
gave the Belgians a frightful scare. One shell landed in the
middle of the Palace Hotel on the beach of Ostend. That was
the only damage. Luckily, it was an English establishment
which they themselves demolished.

We flew that evening with a vengeance. During one of our
flights in the large battle plane we had gone very far out to
sea. The aircraft had two engines, and we experimented with
a new steering device that would make it possible to fly a
straight course with only one engine. When we were somewhat far out, I saw beneath us, not on the water, but—as it
appeared to me—a ship sailing under the water, even though
I could see it as if it were above water. I brought this to
Zeumer's attention, and we went lower to look more closely.
I am not enough of a naval man to say what it was; but it was
clear that it was a submarine. But of what nationality? That
is a doubly difficult question, which, in my opinion, only a
naval man can solve—and then not always. One can hardly
recognize color, much less a flag. Besides, a submarine does
not have such things underwater. We carried two bombs, and
I was in a quandary: Should I drop them or not? The submarine had not seen us because it was half underwater. We
could have flown calmly above it and waited for the moment
it surfaced for air to drop our eggs. That is certainly a very
critical point for our sister service. When we had fooled
around quite a while with the fellows down below, I suddenly
noticed that the water was gradually disappearing from our
radiator. I did not like that and brought it to the attention of

my pilot. He made a long face and prepared to go home. However, we were roughly twenty kilometers from the coast, and first we had to fly that distance. The engine began to quit, and I quietly prepared myself for a cold and damp bath. But we made it The old barge managed with one engine and the new steering device, and we were able to reach the coast and land very nicely at our field.

One must have luck. If we had not experimented with the new steering device that day, we would have been lost beyond hope.

A Drop of Blood for the Fatherland

(OSTEND)

I have never really been wounded. At the critical moment I always bent my head or drew in my belly. I have often wondered why I have not been hit. Once a shot went through both of my fur-lined boots; another time, through my scarf; and once, along my arm through the fur and leather of my jacket. But I was never touched.

One fine day we flew our large battle plane to entertain the English with our bombs. We reached the target and dropped the first bombs. It is, naturally, very interesting to watch the results of such a mission. At least one always likes to see the explosion. But my large battle plane, which was well-suited for carrying bombs, had a stupid peculiarity that made it hard to see the explosion of the bombs dropped, for immediately after the drop the airplane moved over the target and covered it completely with its wings. This always made me angry, since one had so little fun because of it. When the bomb bursts below and one sees the lovely gray-white cloud of the explosion near the target, it is very pleasing. So I signaled to my good friend Zeumer to fly so the wings were off to the side. In so doing I forgot that my infamous old barge had two propellers which turned right and left near my observer seat. I was showing him approximately where the bomb had hit, and —smack!—one of my fingers had been hit. I was surprised at first, but Zeumer had noticed nothing.

I was sick of dropping bombs and quickly let the last one go and made for home.

My love for the large battle plane, which at best had been weak, suffered seriously from this bomb drop. I could not fly again for a week. Now my finger has only a scratch, but at least I can say with pride: "I, too, have a war wound."

My First Aerial Combat

(1 SEPTEMBER 1915)

Zeumer and I would have been only too glad to have a fight in the air. Naturally, we were flying our large battle plane. The name of our barge (*Grosskampfflugzeug*) alone gave us such courage that we felt it would be impossible for an opponent to elude us.

We flew from five to six hours a day without ever seeing an Englishman. It was quite discouraging. One morning on patrol I suddenly discovered a Farman flying reconnaissance, completely unaware of our presence. My heart beat furiously as Zeumer approached him. I was excited about what would happen. I had never seen an aerial combat, and I had only a vague conception of it—somewhat as you do now, my dear reader.

Before I knew what was happening, both of us, the Englishman and us, were rushing toward each other. I had gotten, at best, four shots off when the Englishman suddenly got behind us and shot the whole works at us. I must say I did not have the feeling of danger, because I could not really predict the final result of such a battle. We turned time and again around each other until, finally, to our great surprise, the Englishman turned away from us and flew off. I was greatly disappointed, and so was my pilot.

Arriving home, we were both in a very bad mood. He blamed me for having shot badly, and I blamed him for not having brought me into a good firing position—in short, our aviation rapport, which was so splendid before, had suffered badly.

We examined our crate and saw that it had taken a respectable number of hits.

On the same day we undertook a second patrol, but it was also without results. I was very depressed, for I had imagined it would be quite different in a *Kampfgeschwader* [battle group]. I had always believed that when I fired, the enemy would fall. But I soon learned that an airplane could endure a great deal. I finally became convinced that no matter how much I shot, it would never come down.

We did not lack courage. Zeumer flew with rare skill, and I was a fairly good shot. We were puzzled. But we were not alone. Even today there are many who find themselves in the same position. The business of flying really needs to be understood.

In the Battle of Champagne

The wonderful time in Ostend was very short, for soon the battle in the Champagne region broke out and we flew to this Front in order to play a greater part with our large battle planes. We soon realized that our old packing crate was a grand airplane, but it would never make a fighter.

Once I flew with Osteroth, whose airplane was somewhat smaller than our old barge. About five kilometers behind the Front we encountered a Farman two-seater. Osteroth calmly approached him, and for the first time I saw an opponent in the air within reasonable distance. Osteroth skillfully flew so close that I could easily bring him under fire. The enemy had not noticed us at all, for he did not begin to return fire until my gun jammed. I shot my cartridge case of a hundred rounds, and then I could not believe my eyes: Suddenly the enemy airplane went down in a curious spiral. I followed it with my eyes and tapped Osteroth on the head. It fell and fell and then dropped into a huge bomb crater; we saw it standing upright, tail pointing to the sky. According to the map, it lay five kilometers behind the Front, on the other side of the lines. At that time airplanes shot down behind enemy lines did not count; otherwise, I would have one more on my victory list today. But I was very proud of my success, for, in other respects, the main thing is that a fellow is brought down, not that one is credited for doing it.

How I Met Boelcke

At this time Zeumer tried out a Fokker "Eindecker," and I had to look on as he sailed over the earth alone. The battle of the Champagne was raging. The French fliers were making themselves noticed. We were assembled into a fighting squadron and left by train on 1 October 1915. In the dining car a young, unpretentious lieutenant sat at the table near mine. There was no reason to take special notice of him except that, of all of us, he was the only one who had shot down four enemy fliers. He had been mentioned by name in the dispatches. He impressed me because his experiences were quite exciting. Even though I had taken great pains, up to that point I had not destroyed a single enemy plane; that is, I had not been credited with any. I wanted to learn how this *Leutnant* Boelcke had really accomplished it. So I asked him: "Tell me honestly, how do you really do it?" He laughed heartily, although I was quite serious. Then he answered me: "Good heavens, it indeed is quite simple. I fly in as close as I can, take good aim, shoot, and then he falls down." I merely shook my head and thought to myself that I had done the same thing but they had not fallen down. The difference was, of course, that he flew a Fokker fighter, and I a large battle plane.

I took the trouble to get better acquainted with this nice, unassuming man who had impressed me so much. We often played cards together and took walks, at which times I would question him. Thus, I decided: "You must learn to fly a Fokker yourself, then perhaps things will be better."

Now my thoughts and aspirations were on how to learn to "work the stick" myself. Previously I had only been an observer. I was soon offered the chance to learn to fly an old crate in the Champagne. I pursued it with great zeal, and after twenty-five hours of flying instruction I was ready for a solo flight.

The First Solo Flight

(10 OCTOBER 1915)

There are few moments in life that produce as nervous a sensation as the first solo flight.

Zeumer, my teacher, announced to me one afternoon: "You

are ready to fly alone." I must say that I would rather have answered: "I am too afraid." But this could never come from a defender of the fatherland. Therefore, good or bad, I had to swallow my cowardice and sit in the machine.

Once again he explained every theory of movement to me. I barely heard what he said, for I was of the firm conviction I would forget half of what he told me.

The engine started with a roar. I gave it the gas and the machine began to pick up speed, and suddenly I could not help but notice that I was really flying. Suddenly it was no longer an anxious feeling, but, rather, one of daring. Now it was all up to me. No matter what happened, I was no longer frightened. With contempt for death I made a wide curve to the left, shut off the engine precisely over the designated tree, and waited to see what would happen now. Then came the most difficult part, the landing. I remembered the essential manipulations; I performed them mechanically. However, the machine reacted differently than when Zeumer sat in it. I lost my balance, made some wrong movements, and landed nose-first with what was once the instruction machine. Sadly I looked at the slight damage, amid laughter from all sides.

Two days later I went to my airplane with mad passion, and suddenly all went wonderfully well.

Two weeks later I was ready to take my first examination. I flew the prescribed figure eight and the ordered number of landings, whereupon I proudly got out of the machine and heard, to my great surprise, that I had failed. There was nothing else to do but try once more to pass the first examination.

(A LETTER)

Réthel, 2 November 1915

The flying gloves have just arrived. You can scarcely imagine how happy I am with them. My sincere thanks for them.

As you well know, I like variety very much, so you will certainly not wonder when I tell you that I am getting ready to leave the beautiful Champagne country in the near future. I have received orders to fly a *Riesenflugzeug* [giant airplane], but, unfortunately, it is not ready yet. Therefore, my pilot, Herr Von Osteroth, and I must go to Berlin in order to become familiar with the giant barge. It can hold almost as many bombs as a Zeppelin. Five or six men fly in it: mechanic, machine-gunner, two pilots, and an observer. I am very curious about the crate. Hopefully, we will see each other more often. Nevertheless, you ought to come to Berlin now.

My Training at Döberitz

In order to get through my examinations I had to go to Berlin. I took advantage of an opportunity to fly as an observer in a giant airplane going to Berlin, where I received orders to Döberitz (15 November 1915). From the beginning I took an interest in the giant airplane. It is funny, but as a result of flying the giant airplane it became clear to me that only the smallest airplane would serve my purpose as a combat pilot. Such a big barge is not responsive enough for combat, and that is the main thing in my business.

The difference between the large battle plane and the giant airplane is that the giant airplane is considerably larger and is more suitable for bombing and less for fighting.

I went through my examinations in Döberitz with a charming fellow, *Oberleutnant* Bodo Freiherr von Lyncker. We got on very well together, had the same passion and the same views about our future work. Our objective was to fly Fokkers in a *Jagdstaffel* [Fighter Squadron] on the Western Front. A year later we were able to work together, although only for a short time, as my good friend caught a fatal bullet while shooting down his third airplane.[7]

We had many fine times in Döberitz. For example, one of these involved "off-field landings." I used this opportunity to combine the necessary with the agreeable. My favorite off-field landing place was the Buchow Estate, where I was well-known. I had been invited to hunt wild pigs there, and this was rather compatible with my duty, for on nice evenings I would have preferred to fly, except for my passion for hunting. Therefore, I arranged my off-field landing place so that I could comfortably reach my hunting grounds.

I took a second pilot with me as an observer, and sent him back in the evening. During the night I set out after the pigs, and the next morning this pilot would fetch me again.

If I had not been fetched, I would have been in trouble, as I would have had to march ten kilometers. So I needed a man who would fetch me from my high perch in any weather. But not everyone will fly in foul weather; yet, I found one hearty, daring fellow.

One morning after I had spent the night outside, a tremendous snowstorm began. One could not see more than fifty meters. It was just eight o'clock, the designated time the pilot was to pick me up. I silently hoped this time he would not come. But suddenly I heard a buzzing—although I could see nothing—and five minutes later the airplane lay in front of me, all twisted out of shape.

First Time as a Pilot

On Christmas Day, 1915, I took my third examination. In connection with it, I flew to Schwerin, where I visited the Fokker factory. I took my mechanic with me as observer, and

[7] 18 February 1917

later flew with him from Berlin to Breslau, from Breslau to Schweidnitz, from Schweidnitz to Lüben, from Lüben to Berlin, landing in-between to look up relatives and acquaintances. As an old observer, it was not hard to find my way.

In March I was with *Kampfgeschwader* 2 at Verdun and learned aerial combat as a pilot—that is, I learned how to handle the airplane in battle. I was then flying a two-seater.

My accomplishments are mentioned in the Army Report of 26 April 1916, although I am not personally named. I had had a machine gun mounted between the wings of my airplane, like the Nieuport, and was very proud of this construction. People laughed at it because it looked very primitive. Naturally, I had absolute confidence in it and soon had the opportunity to use it practically.

I met a Nieuport which, apparently, was also flown by a beginner, because he acted foolishly fearful. I flew toward him, whereupon he flew away. Evidently his gun had jammed. It didn't seem that I would be able to engage him. On the contrary, I thought: "What would happen if you shot at him?" I flew after him, and for the first time, from an ever closing distance, squeezed the button of the machine gun—a short series of well-aimed shots, and the Nieuport reared up and rolled over. At first my observer and I believed it was one of the many tricks the Frenchmen go in for. But this "trick" did not stop; he went down lower and lower. Then my observer tapped my helmet and called out: "I congratulate you, he is falling!" In fact, he fell in a forest behind Fort Douaumont and disappeared among the trees. It was clear to me that I had shot him down. But—on the other side! I flew home and reported nothing more than "an aerial combat, one Nieuport shot down." A day later I read of my heroic deed in the Army Report. I was very proud of it, but this Nieuport is not counted among the number I brought down.

ARMY REPORT OF 26 APRIL 1916

Two enemy airplanes were shot down in aerial combat over Fleury, southwest of Douaumont.[8]

Death of Holck

(30 APRIL 1916)

As a neophyte pilot, I was once on a pursuit flight over Fort Douaumont when it was under fierce bombardment. I watched a German Fokker attacking three Caudrons. But, to my misfortune, there was a strong west wind. During the course of the battle the German was driven over the city of Verdun. I brought this to the attention of my observer, who was of the opinion that he must be quite a plucky fellow. We wondered if it could be Boelcke, and we wanted to go there to find out. But then I saw, to my horror, that the attacker became the defender. The Frenchmen, whose strength had meanwhile been increased by at least ten airplanes, were forcing the German lower and lower. I could not come to his help because I was too far from the fighting and, besides, my heavy machine could not overcome the wind. The Fokker defended himself desperately. Now the enemy had driven him down to at least six hundred meters. Then suddenly his pursuers renewed their attack. He disappeared in a dive into a

[8] Although not credited with the victory, Von Richthofen's Nieuport was listed in the official report as one of the two enemy planes shot down that day.

cumulus cloud. I breathed easier, for in my view that was his salvation.

When I returned home I reported what I had seen and learned that the unfortunate pilot was Holck, my old comrade in arms from the Eastern Front, who had become a fighter pilot shortly before the Verdun offensive.

Count von Holck had plunged straight down with a shot through the head. That event affected me deeply, for he was not merely a model of energy; he was also a man of rare personality.

A Flight in a Thunderstorm

Our activity at Verdun was interrupted in the summer of 1916 by frequent thunderstorms, and nothing is more disagreeable to a flier than to have to fly through a thunderstorm. During the battle of the Somme, for example, a whole English squadron landed behind our lines because they had been surprised by a thunderstorm. They were taken prisoner.

I had never made an attempt to fly through a thunderstorm, but I could not resist experimenting once. Thunder was in the air the whole day. From my airfield at Mont I had flown over to the vicinity of Metz in order to settle some things. Then the following happened on my flight home:

I was at the airfield in Metz and wanted to return to my field. As I pulled my machine out of the hangar the first signs of an approaching thunderstorm became noticeable. The wind blew up the sand, and a pitch-black wall arose from the north. Old, experienced pilots urged me not to fly. But I had already promised to come back, and I would have appeared timid if I stayed away because of a stupid thunderstorm. Therefore, I decided to give it the gas and try it once! Right at the start it began to rain. I had to take off my goggles in order to see anything. The trouble was that I had to go over the Moselle Mountains, straight through the valleys where the thunderstorm was raging. I thought to myself, "You will be lucky to get through," and got closer and closer to the black clouds which reached down to the earth. I flew as low as possible, and in doing so, I had to jump over houses and rows of trees. I no longer knew where I was. The storm seized my airplane as if it were a mere piece of paper and tossed it around. My heart sank lower. I could no longer land in the mountains. Therefore, I had to go on.

All around me it was black. Beneath me the trees bent under the storm. Suddenly a wooded height appeared before me. I had to go over it, and as luck would have it, my good Albatros got me over. I could only fly straight ahead, taking every obstacle that came along in turn. It was like riding a steeplechase over trees, villages, church towers, and chimneys. I could fly no higher than five meters, in order to avoid the black thunderclouds. Lightning flashed all around me. At the time, I did not know that lightning cannot strike an airplane. I believed that death would come at any moment, and surely the storm would throw me into a village or forest. If the engine had quit, I would have been done for.

Then suddenly I saw a light place in front of me. The storm had already passed there; if I could reach this point, I would be saved. Gathering all of my energy, as only a frivolous man can, I steered toward the light.

Suddenly, as if wrenched out, I was free of the thunderclouds. I flew through streaming rain, but otherwise I was out of danger.

Despite the pouring rain, I landed at my own airfield, where everyone waited anxiously for me. A report had come from Metz as soon as I departed that I had disappeared in a thundercloud on the way out.

Never again, unless demanded by my fatherland, will I fly through a thunderstorm. But in recollection, everything was beautiful. There were some exhilarating moments that I would not have wanted to miss in my flying life.

First Time in a Fokker

From the beginning of my career as a pilot I had only one ambition, and that was to fly a single-seat fighter plane. After annoying my commander for a long time, I finally received permission to go up in a Fokker. The rotary engine revolving with the propeller was entirely new to me. Also, it was quite strange to sit alone in a small airplane.

I shared this Fokker with a friend named Reimann, who is now long dead. I flew it in the morning, while he flew it in the afternoon. Each was afraid the other would smash the crate. On the second day we flew against the enemy. I encountered no Frenchmen in the morning, and it was Reimann's turn in the afternoon. He did not return from his flight. However, there was no report of his falling—nothing. Later in the evening the infantry reported an aerial engagement, between a Nieuport and a German Fokker, during the course of which the German apparently landed on the other side of no man's land. It could only be Reimann, for all the others had come back. We felt sorry for our brave comrade, then later that night a telephone report came in saying a German flying officer had suddenly appeared at the farthest trenches of an infantry position in no man's land. It turned out to be Reimann. His engine had been shot to pieces and he had had to make a forced landing. He had landed between the lines but could not reach our side. He quickly set fire to the machine and then hid himself in a bomb crater several hundred meters away. During the night he crawled along the ground until he reached our trenches. Thus ended our first joint venture, "The Fokker."

Some weeks later we received a second machine. This time I felt obligated to dispatch it into the Great Beyond. It was perhaps my third flight with the small, fast machine. The engine quit on take-off, and I was suddenly forced to land in a hayfield. In a flash the once proud, beautiful machine was an unrecognizable mass. It was a wonder nothing happened to me.

(A LETTER)

Before Verdun, 27 April 1916
In great haste, joyful tidings: Look at the Army Report of 26 April 1916! My machine gun is responsible for one of two airplanes mentioned.

(A LETTER)

Before Verdun, 3 May 1916
Very sincere thanks for your kind wishes on my birthday, which I spent very pleasantly here. In the morning I had three very nerve-wracking aerial combats, and in the evening I sat with Zeumer, my first pilot, until one o'clock in the morning with a bowl of punch under a blossoming apple tree. I feel very content with my new occupation as a fighter pilot; I believe that no post in the war is as attractive as this one. I am flying a Fokker, which is the airplane with which Boelcke and Immelmann have had their tremendous successes. I am sorry about the death of Holck. Three days before he fell I visited him and we had a good time together. He told me of his im-

prisonment in Montenegro. It is hard to think that this healthy and vigorously powerful man is no longer with us. I was an eyewitness to his last air battle. First he shot down one Frenchman from among a squadron of them, then apparently had a jam in his gun and tried to fly back to our lines. Then a whole swarm of Frenchmen pursued him. With a shot through the head he tumbled down from three thousand me-ters—a fine death. Holck with only one arm or one leg would be unthinkable. Today I fly to his funeral.

(A LETTER)

Before Verdun, 22 June 1916

What do you think of Immelmann's death? In the long run everyone believes it—even Boelcke. The commander of Lothar's squadron has also not returned from a photorecon-naissance. A day before, the commander of my old *Kampsgeschwader* 1 (known at the time as *Brieftauben Abteilung, Ostende*) was shot down. He was Ernst Freiherr von Gers-dorff, probably the most qualified commander a battle squad-ron ever had. I always liked him very much.

(A LETTER)

Before Verdun, 6 July 1916

A few days ago I crashed my Fokker right on its nose. Wit-nesses were more than a little surprised when I crawled out of the wreckage completely unhurt. My good friend Georg Zeumer has already gone me one better. First he was shot down by the French, and three days later he broke his thigh under quite stupid circumstances.

I am entertaining the idea of going to Boelcke to become a student of his. I always need a change. That would be something new again, and not to my detriment either.

Bombing Flights in Russia

In June we were suddenly ordered to move out. We did not know where we were going, but we had a good idea. When our commander finally announced that we were going to Russia, we were not overly amazed. We traveled through the whole of Germany on a train consisting of dining and sleeping cars until we finally came to Kovel. There we stayed in our railway cars. Living in trains has many advantages, of course; one is continually ready to travel on, and one always has the same quarters. But a sleeping car is the most dreadful thing there is in the heat of the Russian summer. For that reason I agreed to go with two good friends, Gerstenberg and Scheele, into a nearby forest at Kovel, where we erected a tent and lived like gypsies. That was a lovely time.

In Russia our battle squadron dropped many bombs. We busied ourselves with angering the Russians and dropped our "eggs" on their finest railway installations. On one of these days our whole squadron set out to bomb a very important train station called Manjewicze, about thirty kilometers behind the Front. The Russians were planning an attack, so this station was filled with trains standing side by side. A whole stretch of track was covered with engines and cars. From the air one could see troop trains at every switch. It was really a worthwhile target.

There are many things to be enthusiastic about in flying, and for a while I was much interested in bombing. It gave me a sinister pleasure to plaster our "friends"[9] down below. I often went out twice a day on such flights. This day Manjewicze was the target. Each squadron made preparations to set out against the Russians.

The machines stood ready and each pilot tested his engine, for it is a painful thing to be forced to land on the wrong side of the Front, especially in Russia. The Russians are terrible to captured fliers. If they catch one they will certainly kill him. That is the one danger in Russia, for they have no fliers of their own, or as good as none at all. If a Russian flier appeared, he was sure to have bad luck and be shot down by his own men. The antiaircraft guns in Russia are often quite good, but their number is not sufficient. Compared to the Western Front, in any case, flying on the Eastern Front is like a holiday.

The machines rolled with difficulty to the starting line. They were filled to capacity with bombs. Many times I hauled one-hundred-fifty-kilogram bombs with a normal C-type airplane. I have even had with me heavy observers, who had apparently not suffered from the meat shortage, as well as two machine guns, although I never got to try them out in Russia. It is a shame that there is not a Russian in my collection of victories. His cockade would look very picturesque on the wall. To get back to the main point, a flight with a heavily laden, clumsy machine is not easy, especially in the afternoon heat. On the take-off run, the planes sway very uncomfortably. They do not falter, of course; the one-hundred-fifty "horses" see to that. But it is not a pleasant feeling to have so much explosive material and gasoline along. At last one is in a calm sea of air, and gradually comes to enjoy the bombing flight. It is beautiful to fly straight ahead, with a definite target and firm orders. After a bombing flight one has the feeling he has accomplished

[9] Von Richthofen referred to the enemy in this jovial way.

something, whereas many times on a pursuit flight, when one has shot down nothing, you reproach yourself with the feeling that you could have done better. I liked dropping bombs. Gradually my observer had gotten the knack of flying perpendicular to the target, and, with the help of an aiming telescope, he waited for the right moment to lay his eggs.

The flight to Manjewicze was beautiful. I made it often. We flew over gigantic complexes of forests in which elk and lynx certainly must roam. To be sure, the villages looked as if only foxes could live in them. The only large village in the whole area was Manjewicze. Around the village countless tents were pitched, and by the train station were innumerable huts. We could not make out the sign of the Red Cross. A squadron had been there before us. One could determine this solely by the smoking houses and huts. They had not done badly. The one exit of the train station was obviously blocked by a lucky hit. The locomotive was still steaming. The engineer was probably hid in a dugout somewhere. On the other side of the town a locomotive was coming out at three-quarter speed. Of course, I could not resist to temptation to attack. We flew toward the engine and dropped a bomb a hundred meters in front of it. The desired result was obtained: The locomotive had stopped and could not move. We turned and neatly dropped bomb after bomb, finely aimed through the telescope sight, on the train station. We had plenty of time and no one bothered us. An enemy airfield was in the vicinity, but its pilots were not to be seen. Antiaircraft shells burst sporadically but in a different direction than where we were flying. We saved a bomb for use on the flight home. Then we saw an enemy flier as he started from his field. Did he plan to attack us? I don't think so. More than likely he sought security in the air, for during a bombing flight over an airfield the air is certainly the most comfortable place to be to avoid personal danger.

We took a roundabout way home and looked for troop encampments. It was special fun to harass the gentlemen below with our machine guns. Such half-civilized tribes as the Asiatics are more afraid of such things than the refined Englishmen. It is especially interesting to shoot at enemy cavalry. It causes an enormous commotion among the men. They rush off to all points of the compass. I would not like to be the commander of a Cossack squadron shot up by fliers with machine guns.

Soon we saw our lines again. Now it was time to get rid of our last bomb. We decided to present a bomb to a captive balloon, the only captive balloon the Russians had. We descended smoothly to a few hundred meters from the balloon. They had begun to reel it in with great haste, but as the bomb was falling, the reeling stopped. I do not believe I hit it but, rather, that the Russians in their panic had left their officer in the lurch up in the basket and had all run away.

We finally reached our own lines and, after arriving back home, were somewhat surprised to find that one of the wings showed a hit.

Another time we were in the same area preparing to attack the Russian troops about to cross the Stokhod River. We approached the dangerous place laden with bombs and plenty of ammunition for the machine guns. On arriving, we saw to our great astonishment that the enemy cavalry was already crossing the Stokhod. One single bridge served as the crossing point. It was clear that if this was hit, it would hurt the enemy advance tremendously. There was a thick mass of troops trundling over the narrow footbridge. We went down to the lowest possible altitude and observed that the enemy cavalry was crossing with great speed. The first bomb burst not far from them; the second and third followed directly after it. There was immediate confusion and disorder below. The bridge itself had not been hit; nevertheless, traffic was completely stopped and everything that had legs used them, taking off in all directions. That was quite a successful attack, for it cost only three bombs; besides, another squadron was coming behind us. So we could proceed to other targets. My observer fired the machine gun continually at the chaps down below, and it was wild fun. How successful we were, I cannot say, of course. The Russians have not told me either. But I imagine that it was our plane alone that had repelled the Russian attack.

Boelcke!

The August sun was almost overpowering on the sandy airfield in Kovel. We were talking among ourselves when someone said: "Today the great Boelcke comes to visit us, or, rather, his brother in Kovel." That evening the famous man appeared and, much to our pleasure, told us many interesting things about his journey to Turkey, from where he was returning in order to report to Headquarters. He spoke of going back to the Somme to continue his work and of setting up a whole *Jagdstaffel*.[10] For this purpose he was selecting men from the Flying Service who appeared to be suitable. I dared not ask him to take me with him. I did not want to leave our squadron on the basis of its being too boring—On the contrary, we made long and interesting flights, and peppered many a Russki train station with our bombs—but the thought of fighting again on the Western Front appealed to me. There is nothing finer for a young cavalry officer than flying off on a hunt.

[10] Fighter squadron

Boelcke was to leave early the next day. I heard a knock on my door early in the morning, and there he stood, a big man wearing the *Pour le mérite,* Germany's highest award. I didn't rightly know what to say. I didn't dare think that he might have selected me to be one of his pupils. I almost hugged him when he asked me if I wanted to go with him to the Somme. Three days later I was on the train traveling across Germany to my new field. My ardent wish was fulfilled, and the most wonderful time of my life began. I dared not hope at the time that it would turn out as successful as it has. Upon leaving, a good friend called to me: "Don't come back without the *Pour le mérite!*"

My First Englishman

(17 SEPTEMBER 1916)

We lined up at the firing range and fired our machine guns one after another down the line. The day before we had received our new airplanes, and the next morning Boelcke was to fly with us. We were all beginners; none of us had previously been credited with a success. Whatever Boelcke told us was taken as gospel. We knew that in the last few days he had shot down at least one Englishman a day, and many times two every morning.

The morning of the seventeenth of September was a wonderful day. We could rely on brisk English flying activity. Before we took off, Boelcke gave us precise instructions, and then for the first time we flew as a squadron under the leadership of the famous man whom we followed without question.

We had just arrived at the Front when we spotted the flank bursts of our antiaircraft guns. An enemy squadron was right over our lines flying in the direction of Cambrai. Of course, Boelcke was the first to see them, for he saw more than most men. Soon we, too, grasped the situation, and each of us strained to stay close behind Boelcke. It was clear to all of us that we had to pass our first examination under the eyes of our revered leader. We approached the enemy squadron slowly, but it could no longer escape us. We were between the Front and the enemy. If he wanted to go back, he would have to go by us. We counted seven enemy airplanes, and opposed them with only five. All the Englishmen flew great two-seat bomber airplanes. We were only seconds away from the beginning of the fight. Boelcke was the first one to get near the skin of the cursed enemy, but he did not shoot. I was the second, and my comrades were close to me. The Englishman near me was a big, dark-colored barge. I did not ponder long and took aim at him. He shot and I shot, but we both missed. The fight then began. I tried to get behind him because I could only shoot in the direction I was flying. This was not necessary for him, as his observer's rotating machine gun could reach all sides. But this fellow was no beginner, for he knew very well that the moment I succeeded in getting behind him, his last hour would be sounded. At the time I did not have the conviction I have now that "he must fall," but, rather, I was much more anxious to see *if* he would fall, and that is a significant difference. After the first or the second or third miss, it occurs to one: "So that's how you do it."

My Englishman twisted and turned, crossing my line of fire. It did not occur to me that there were other Englishmen in the squadron who could come to the aid of their hard-pressed comrade. There was only the growing thought: "He must fall, come what may!" Then, finally, there was a brief but advantageous moment. The enemy had apparently lost sight of me and flew straight ahead. In a fraction of a second I was sitting on his tail. I gave him a short burst from my machine gun. I was so close I was afraid I would ram him.

Then, suddenly, his propeller turned no more. Hit! The engine was probably shot to pieces, and he would have to land near our lines. Reaching his own positions was out of the question. I noticed the machine swaying from side to side; something was not quite right with the pilot. Also, the observer was not to be seen, his machine gun pointed unattended up in the air. I had no doubt hit him also, and he must have been lying on the floor of the fuselage.

The Englishman landed near the airfield used by a neighboring squadron. I was so excited that I could not resist coming down, and I landed with such eagerness on this strange field that I almost went over on my nose. I landed near the Englishman and jumped out of my airplane. A group of soldiers was already streaming toward the fallen enemy. Arriving there, I found that my assumption was correct. The engine was shot to pieces, and both crewmen were severely wounded. The observer had died instantly, and the pilot died while being transported to the nearest field hospital. Later I erected a gravestone to the memory of my honorably fallen enemies.

When I came home, Boelcke was already sitting with my other comrades at breakfast and wondering where I had been so long. I proudly reported for the first time: "One Englishman shot down!" Everyone rejoiced, for I was not the only victor. Besides Boelcke, who, as usual, had his breakfast victory, every one of the beginners had gained their first aerial victories.

Since that day, no English squadron has dared to venture near Cambrai as long as *Jagdstaffel Boelcke* was there.

The Battle of the Somme

I have never found a more beautiful hunting ground than in the skies at the battle of the Somme. The first Englishmen came very early in the morning, and the last disappeared long after the sun had gone down. "An El Dorado for fighter pilots," Boelcke once said. That was when Boelcke had increased his victories from twenty to forty in but two months. We beginners did not have the experience that our master did, and we were happy enough when we ourselves did not catch a thrashing. But it was wonderful! Not a mission without an air fight. Often great air battles of forty to sixty Englishmen against, unfortunately, fewer Germans. They did it with quantity, and we did it with quality.

But the Englishman is a plucky fellow—we must allow him that. He came back and forth at quite low altitudes and visited Boelcke at his field with bombs. He formally challenged us to battle and constantly accepted it as well. I have scarcely met an Englishman who would refuse a fight, while the Frenchman prefers to painfully avoid every encounter with the enemy.

It was a wonderful time at our squadron. The spirit of the leader spread to his pupils. We could blindly trust his leadership. There was no possibility that anyone would be left behind. The thought never came to us. And so we roamed bright and merry, diminishing our enemies.

On the day Boelcke fell, the squadron had already scored forty victories. Now it has over a hundred. The spirit of Boelcke lives on among his able successors.

(A LETTER)

At the Somme, 5 October 1916
On the thirtieth of September I shot down my third Englishman. He plunged down in flames. One's heart beats faster if the opponent, whose face he has just seen, plunges burn-

ing from four thousand meters. Arriving below, I found very little remaining of either the men or the machine. I took a small piece of the insignia from this one as a souvenir. I had taken the machine gun from my second to also keep as a souvenir; it had a bullet of mine in the bolt, which rendered it useless. My Frenchman from Verdun does not count on my list of victories, unfortunately. Earlier in the war one received the *Pour le mérite* after his eighth victory, but no longer, even though it is becoming ever more difficult to shoot down an enemy plane. In the last four weeks since the founding of *Jagdstaffel Boelcke,* we have lost five of our ten airplanes.

Death of Boelcke

On the twenty-eighth of October we flew once again under the leadership of the great man. We always felt secure when he was along. There was only one Boelcke. The weather was very stormy, with many clouds. Other pilots did not fly that day, only fighter pilots.

From a great distance we saw two impudent Englishmen over the Front, apparently having fun in the bad weather. We were six against their two. If they had been twenty we would not have been surprised to receive the signal of attack from Boelcke.

The usual battle began. Boelcke went after one, and I the other. Close to Boelcke flew a good friend of his. It was an interesting fight. Both fired, and at any moment the Englishman had to fall. Suddenly an unnatural movement was observed in both German airplanes. The thought flashed through my brain: collision! I had never seen a collision in the air, although, like many others, I had imagined it. But this was not a collision; rather, it was a mere touching. But at the great speed of an airplane, even a slight touching is a violent concussion.

Boelcke immediately pulled away from his intended victim and fell to earth in great spiraling curves. I still did not have the feeling he would crash, but as he glided below I noticed that a section of his wings was broken. I could not observe what happened next, but in the clouds he lost a whole wing. His airplane became uncontrollable and he plunged down, accompanied all the way by his faithful friend.[11] When we got home, the report was already there: "Our Boelcke is dead!" One could hardly conceive of it.

It was most grievous, of course, to the one who survived the accident.

It is strange that everyone who came to know Boelcke imagined he was his one true friend. I have met about forty of these "one true" friends of Boelcke, and each imagined that he indeed was *the* one true friend. Men whose names Boelcke never knew believed they were especially close to him. It was a strange phenomenon that I have observed only in Boelcke. He never had a personal enemy. He was equally friendly to everyone, no more to one, no less to another.

The one who was perhaps closest to Boelcke was the one who collided with him.

The Eighth

In Boelcke's time, eight victories was quite a respectable number. Those who hear of the colossal numbers of victories nowadays must think that shooting down airplanes is becoming

[11] Erwin Böhme, who later commanded *Jasta* 2, from 23 November 1916 to his death on 29 November 1917

easier. I can only assure them that it is becoming more difficult from month to month; indeed, from week to week. Of
course, there are more opportunities now, but, unfortunately,
the armament of the enemy is getting better and his numbers
are getting larger. When Max Immelmann shot down his
first opponent, he had the good fortune to find an enemy who
had no machine gun at all. Such novice aviators are now
found only over Johannistal.[12] On the ninth of November
1916 I flew against the enemy with my comrade in arms, the
eighteen-year-old Hans Imelmann.[13]

We were together in *Jagdstaffel Boelcke,* although we had
met before that, and had always gotten along very well. Comradeship is most important. I already had seven victories,
Imelmann five, which was quite a lot at the time.

We were at the Front a short time when we saw an enemy
bomber squadron flying along impudently. They came in
tremendous numbers, just as during the Somme battle. I believe there were about forty to fifty in the squadron, although I cannot give the exact number. They had picked a
target not far from our airfield. Shortly before they reached
the target, I reached the bomber in the rear position of the
enemy formation. My first shots put his gunner out of action
and probably tickled the pilot as well; in any case, he decided
to land with his bombs. I burned him a bit around the edges,
and the haste with which he sought to reach the ground was
most noticeable; that is to say, he plunged down and fell near
our airfield at Lagnicourt.

At the same time, Imelmann was similarly involved in a
fight with an Englishman, whom he also brought down in the
same area. We quickly flew home so we could view the
machines we had shot down. We drove in a car to the vicinity

12 Location of an aviation training school in Germany

13 The names Max Immelmann and Hans Imelmann have two distinct
spellings.

of my opponent's crash, and then had to run a great distance across many acres. It was very hot, so I unbuttoned everything, even my shirt and collar. I took the jacket off and left my cap in the car, instead, I took a knotty walking stick with me, as my boots were in mud up to the knees. I looked like a tramp when I came to the spot where my victim was. Naturally, an enormous number of men had gathered around it.

A group of officers stood on the other side. I went over to them, greeted them and asked the first one I met if he could tell me how the air fight had looked, for it is always very interesting afterwards to hear from others looking from the ground how the air battle had looked. I learned that the other English airplanes had dropped their bombs, but that this airplane was still fully armed. The gentleman in question took me by the arm, went over to the group of other officers, quickly asked my name and introduced me to the gentlemen. That was unpleasant, for, as I said, I had mussed my clothes. And the gentlemen whom I was now to meet were all splendidly dressed. I was introduced to an obviously important personage. He wore a general's trousers and a decoration around his neck, but he had a comparatively young-looking face and indefinable shoulder epaulettes—in short, I sensed something out of the ordinary, and buttoned up my shirt and collar in the course of conversation and took on a more military bearing. I did not know who he was. I took leave of him again and went home. In the evening the telephone rang and I learned that he was His Royal Highness the Duke of Saxe-Coburg-Gotha. I was commanded to appear before him. It was known that the Englishmen intended to bomb his headquarters. To that end I had helped keep the assailants away from it. For that reason I received the Saxe-Coburg-Gotha Medal for Bravery.

Major Hawker

I was very proud when I heard that the Englishman I had shot down on the twenty-third of November 1916 was the man we called "The English Immelmann": Major Lanoe G. Hawker.

I was on patrol that day and observed three Englishmen who had nothing else in mind than to hunt. I noticed how they ogled me, and since I felt ready for battle, I let them come. I was lower than the Englishmen; consequently, I had to wait until they came down to me. It did not take long before one dove for me, trying to catch me from behind. After a burst of five shots the sly fellow had to stop, for I was already in a sharp left curve. The Englishman attempted to get behind me while I attempted to get behind him. So it went, both of us flying like madmen in a circle, with engines running full out at three-thousand-meter altitude. First left, then right, each intent on getting above and behind the other. I was soon acutely aware that I was not dealing with a beginner, for he did not dream of breaking off the fight. He had a very maneuverable crate, but mine climbed better, and I finally succeeded in coming in above and behind him.

We had by this time come down to two thousand meters without having reached an outcome, and my opponent must have realized that it was now high time for him to make himself scarce. The wind was working in my favor and we were circling more and more over our positions until finally we were nearly over Bapaume, about a kilometer behind our Front. My opponent waved to me quite cheerfully as we were at a thousand meters altitude as if to say: "Well, well, how do you do?"

The circles that we made around each other were so narrow

that I estimated them to be not further than eighty to a hundred meters. I had time to view my opponent. I peered perpendicularly at him in his cockpit and could observe every movement of his head. If he had not had his flying helmet on, I could have seen what kind of face he made.

Gradually this got to be too much for the brave sportsman, and he finally had to decide whether to land on our side or fly back to his own lines. Naturally, he attempted the latter, after trying in vain to evade me through looping and such tricks. In so doing, my first bullets flew by his ears, for prior to that I had not fired a shot. At about a hundred meters altitude he tried to escape toward the Front by flying zigzag, making his plane a difficult target to hit.

It was now the given moment for me. I followed him from fifty down to thirty meters altitude, firing steadily. The Englishman had to fall. A jam in my guns almost cost me success.

About fifty meters behind our lines he plunged down with a shot through the head. His machine gun was pulled out of the ground and now graces the entrance over the door to my house.

(A LETTER)

Staffel Boelcke, 25 November 1916

For your birthday I send you my most sincere good wishes and the hope that this will be your last wartime birthday. My eleventh Englishman is Major Hawker, twenty-six years old and commander of an English squadron. Prisoners have said he was "the English Boelcke." It was the most difficult battle I have had, but I finally shot him down. Unfortunately, three days ago we lost our leader,[14] and eight days ago an airplane of our squadron as well.

[14] *Oberleutnant* Stephan Kirmaier, who succeeded Boelcke as Commanding Officer of *Jagdstaffel* 2

Pour le mérite[15]

My sixteenth foe had fallen. Consequently, I was the leading fighter pilot. This was the goal I wanted to achieve. A year ago, when we were in training, my friend Bodo von Lyncker asked me: "What is your goal? What would you like to achieve as a flier?" In jest I had answered: "Well, it must be quite nice to be the leading fighter pilot." Neither I nor anyone else believed I would come to that. Boelcke, when asked, "Who looks like he would be a good fighter pilot?" is supposed to have merely said—of course not to me personally, but it was told to me later by another—"That is the man!", pointing his finger at me.

Boelcke and Immelmann had received the *Pour le mérite* with their eighth victories. I had doubled that. What would happen to me? I was very excited. It was whispered I would be given command of a fighter squadron. One day a telegram came, which read: "*Leutnant* von Richthofen designated to be leader of *Jagdstaffel* 11." I must say, I was more annoyed than pleased. I had become so thoroughly acquainted with my comrades in *Jagdstaffel Boelcke* that now to have to begin getting settled anew was irksome. Besides, I would rather have had the *Pour le mérite*.

Two days later—we were cozily sitting together at *Jagdstaffel Boelcke* and celebrating my leaving—a telegram from Headquarters came, saying that His Majesty was graciously presenting me the *Pour le mérite*. Naturally, there was great joy all around. It was a mark of progress.

I had not imagined I would lead a fighter squadron myself, and I never dreamed that one day there would be a *Jagdstaffel Richthofen*.

[15] Nicknamed the "Blue Max" by some English fliers

Jagdstaffel 11, 27 January 1917

You certainly must wonder why I have not written. So much has happened that I do not know what I should write of first. I have been named Commander of *Jagdstaffel* 11 in Douai. Only reluctantly did I leave my beloved *Jagdstaffel Boelcke*. All my resistance did not help me. *Staffel* 11 has been in existence as long as my old unit, only up to now they have not shot down any of the enemy. Working here brings me very little joy at present. The officer corps under me consists of twelve gentlemen.

I was lucky. On my first day here I shot down number seventeen, and on the second day number eighteen. As I shot down my eighteenth, one of my wings broke in two during the air battle at three-hundred-meter altitude. It was only through a miracle that I reached the ground without going *kaput*. On the same day three airplanes of *Jagdstaffel Boelcke* fell. Among them was little Imelmann—a pity! It is not impossible that the same thing that happened to me also happened to them. Unfortunately, I may not come home on leave. I would like to have shown you the *Pour le mérite*.

"Le petit rouge"

One day, for no particular reason, I got the idea to paint my crate glaring red. After that, absolutely everyone knew my red bird. In fact, even my opponents were not completely unaware.

During a fight that occurred at another place on the Front,

I succeeded in shooting down a two-seat Vickers that had been quite calmly photographing our artillery emplacements. My opponent never had a chance to turn and had to hasten to get down to earth, for he had already begun to show suspicious signs of burning. When a plane is in such a condition, we say: "He stinks." As it turned out, in fact, his time was up, for, shortly before the machine came to earth, it burst into bright flames.

I felt a deep compassion for my opponent and decided not to send him plunging down. I wanted to force him to land, for I had the feeling that he was already wounded. He did not fire a shot.

At about five-hundred-meter altitude, a malfunction in my machine during a normal glide also forced me to land before making another turn. Now something quite comical happened. My enemy in his burning machine landed smoothly, while I, the victor, turned over right near him on the barbed wire of the trenches of a reserve emplacement.

A sporting reception followed with both Englishmen, who were more than a little surprised at my crash, for, as I mentioned, they had not fired a shot at me and they could not imagine why I had made a forced landing. These were the first Englishmen I had brought down alive. Therefore, I enjoyed talking with them. Among other things, I asked them if they had ever seen my machine in the air. "Oh yes," one of them said, "I know it quite well. We call it *'Le petit rouge.'"*

Then came what was, in my view, a typically English dirty trick. He asked me why I had acted so carelessly in landing. I told him the reason was that I could not do anything else. Then the scoundrel said that in the last three hundred meters he had attempted to shoot at me, but his guns had·jammed. I had given him a gift of his life. He took it and subsequently repaid me with an insidious personal attack.

Since then I have been unable to again speak with an opponent, for obvious reasons.

(A LETTER)

Jagdstaffel 11

Yesterday I shot down my thirty-first, and my thirtieth the day before. Three days ago I received a direct promotion to *Oberleutnant* [First Lieutenant]. Have therefore gained a good half year. My squadron is doing well. I am very happy with it. Lothar had his first aerial combat yesterday. He was satisfied because the opponent was wounded. We say, "He stunk," because he left a trail of black smoke behind him. The enemy plane did not fall, of course, as that would have been too much luck for the first time. Lothar is very conscientious and will do well. How is Papa and what do you think of yesterday's Army Report?

English and French Aviation

(FEBRUARY 1917)

At this time I was trying to compete with *Jagdstaffel Boelcke.* In the evening we compared our mutual bags. There were some devilish fellows there, and they were never to be outdone. At best, one could but equal them. They already had the advantage of having downed a hundred enemy planes. I must concede this advantage for the present. The chances for victory all depend on which opponent one faces—the sneaky Frenchman or those plucky fellows, the Englishmen. I prefer the Englishmen. The Frenchman flinches, the Englishman seldom does. One can often speak of stupidity here; indeed, the English show this as pluck and daring.

The nice thing about being a fighter pilot is that one does not depend solely on artificial means, but, rather, the decisive factor of victory is simply personal courage. One could be quite a splendid stunt flier and still not be able to shoot down a single airplane. In my opinion, stunting is all a waste of time.

The Frenchman lies in wait for his prey to surprise him in a trap. That is hard to do in the air. Only a beginner will let himself be taken unawares. Ambush does not work, for one cannot hide and the invisible airplane has not yet been invented. Now and then, however, the Gallic blood rages in him and he launches an attack, but it is comparable to carbonated soda. For a moment there is an awful lot of spirit that suddenly goes flat. He is lacking in tenacious endurance.

The Englishman, on the other hand, shows some of his Germanic blood. These sportsmen take readily to flying, but they lose themselves in sport. They have enough amusement looping, diving, flying upside-down and demonstrating similar stunts for our men in the trenches. This would make a good impression during the Johannistal Sportsweek, but the men in the trenches are not as appreciative.

(A LETTER)

Jagdstaffel 11

I intend to come home at the beginning of May, but before that I want to go hunting for wood grouse. I already have an invitation and I'm eager to accept. Then I have been invited to breakfast with the Kaiser. I have now reached number forty-four and will stop at fifty. Lothar already has his tenth aerial victory, and the squadron, since I have been there, had its hundredth.

Shot Down

(MIDDLE OF MARCH 1917)

"Shot down" is really the wrong description of what happened to me. In general, I use the term "shot down" only when one is brought down out of control, but this time I had begun to come down and yet landed intact.

I was with my squadron over our artillery positions in the vicinity of Lens when I saw an opponent who was flying with his squadron. I had to fly quite a way to reach my opponent. That is the most nerve-wracking moment: flying toward the opposition when he has sighted you and there are only a few minutes until the battle begins. I believe that my face becomes pale, but, unfortunately, I never have a mirror with me. I find this exciting moment exquisite—it is extremely stimulating, and I love it all. One sights a flight of planes from afar, recognizes them as the enemy, counts their numbers, and carefully considers the favorable and unfavorable factors. For example, the wind plays an enormous role in the battle as it forces one from our Front or pushes one toward it. I once shot down an Englishman to whom the fatal shot had been given on his side of the enemy lines, and yet he fell near our captive balloons; the wind had carried him that far.

This time we were five; the opposition was three times as strong. The Englishmen flew together like a great swarm of gnats. It is not easy to disperse a group that fly together so well. It is out of the question for one machine to do it, and is even extremely difficult for a larger group, especially when the difference in numbers is unfavorable, as in our case. But one feels so superior to the opponent that he does not doubt for one moment the certainty of success. The spirit of attack and, consequently, the taking of the offensive is the main point in the air as elsewhere. But the opposition thought so, too. I noticed that at once. Scarcely had he seen us, when he immediately turned and headed toward us. Then we were alerted: Look out! Stay together and make it hard for him. We locked together and let the gentlemen come closer. I was on the alert for one of my "friends" to leave the enemy formation. There is always one so stupid. I'm in reach of him. "You are a lost child." I'm on to him with a roar. He has already begun to shoot and is therefore somewhat nervous. I say to myself: "Shoot if you want, you won't hit me." He fires tracer ammunition that obviously goes past me. It is like being in the stream of water pouring from a watering can. It is not pleasant, but the Englishmen fire this damned stuff almost without exception. We have to get used to it, for man is a creature of habit. At this moment I believe I laughed, but I soon learned better.

Now I am almost upon him, about a hundred meters away, the safety catch is off the gun, I aim once to test it, firing some trial shots to see if the guns are in order. This duel cannot last much longer. In my mind I can already see my opponent dropping. The previous excitement is gone. I think quite calmly and objectively now, weighing the probabilities of hitting him and being hit. In all, the fight itself is usually the least exciting, and whoever gets excited makes mistakes. He will never shoot anyone down. But self-control is indeed a matter of habit. At any rate, I do not make a mistake in this fight.

Now I am about fifty meters away, and with some good shots, success cannot fail to come. So I thought! Suddenly there is a loud bang; I have scarcely gotten ten shots off. Again something strikes my machine, and it is clear I have been hit. I'm thankful it's my machine that has been hit and not me. At the same moment there is a frightful stench of fuel, and then the engine slows down. The Englishman notices it, for he shoots even more now. I break off immediately.

I go straight down, instinctively switching the engine off. It was high time to do it. When the fuel tank has been punctured and the stuff is squirting around the legs, the danger of burning is great indeed. Up front there is an engine over one hundred fifty "horses" strong that is glowing hot. A drop of fuel on it and the whole machine goes up in flames. A white mist is trailing in the air behind me. I know it's there from seeing it happen to my opponents. It is the first sign of an explosion. I am three thousand meters up and have a long way to go to get down to earth. Thank God the engine stopped running. I cannot estimate the air speed, but in any case, it is so great that I cannot stick my head out without the rush of air pushing it back in.

Soon I am rid of my opponent and I have time before landing to see what my four other "gentlemen" are doing. They are still engaged in battle. One can hear the machine-gun fire of our opponents, and then our own. Suddenly a rocket. Is it a flare signal of the enemy? No, it is too big for that. It is getting bigger. A machine is burning. But what kind? The machine looks exactly like ours. Thank God it is one of the enemy. Who shot him down? Immediately thereafter a second plane falls from the melee. Like mine, it goes straight down, spinning, always spinning—then it recovers and straightens out. As it flies toward me, I see that it is also an Albatros. Certainly the same thing that happened to me happened to him.

I am still several meters up and have to look around cautiously to see where I can land. This kind of landing does not always go favorably—therefore, watch out. I find a meadow, not very large, but just enough if one sets about landing cautiously. Besides, it is favorable for me, lying directly by the road near Hénin-Liétard. I land there and everything goes smoothly. My first thought is: Where is the other fellow? He landed some kilometers away from me.

I now had time to inspect the damage. There were some other hits, but the one that caused me to break off combat had gone through both fuel tanks. I did not have a drop of fuel in them; the engine was likewise shot up. What a pity, it ran so well.

I let my legs dangle outside the machine and probably made a somewhat foolish face. Immediately a large crowd of soldiers gathered. Then an officer came. He was quite out of breath and very excited, as if something terrible had happened. He rushed up to me, gasping for air, and said: "I hope you are all right. I observed the whole event and I am indeed so excited! Dear God, it looked terrible!" I assured him that nothing was wrong with me at all. Then I jumped down from the airplane and introduced myself. Of course he did not catch a syllable of my name, but he invited me to go with him in his automobile to Hénin-Liétard, where his quarters were. He was an engineering officer.

We were sitting in the car, driving along. My host had still not calmed down. Suddenly he gave a start and asked: "Dear God, where is your driver?" At first I did not quite know what he meant and looked at him somewhat confused. Then it was clear that he took me for the observer of a two-seat airplane and had inquired about my pilot. Quickly I pulled myself together and said flatly: "I drive alone." The word "drive" is despised in the Flying Service. One does not drive, one "flies." I had decidedly sunk in the eyes of this brave gentleman,[16] due to the fact that I "drove" alone. The conversation become somewhat reserved.

[16] Most German two-seater pilots and, indeed, a number of fighter pilots were enlisted men. Hence, they were considered "drivers." This officer probably thought Von Richthofen was an enlisted man, which would account for his sudden reserve.

Then we arrived at his quarters. I still had on my dirty, oily, leather flying jacket and a heavy scarf. Along the way he had of course besieged me with endless questions. Altogether, the gentleman was considerably more excited than I. He compelled me to lie down on his sofa, or he wanted me to, because I must have been flushed from my battle. I assured him that I had already fought in the air many times, but he could not get that into his head. I certainly did not look very warlike.

After some conversation he of course came up with the famous question: "Have you ever shot down an enemy airplane?" As I said before, he had not heard my name. "Oh yes," I said, "now and then." "Indeed. Have you perhaps shot down two?" "No, not two, but twenty-four." He smiled, and repeated his question for me to understand that by "shot down" he meant having it fall down and stay there. I assured him that that was my interpretation of it. Now I was completely looked down on, for he took me for a big braggart. He left me sitting there, saying that we would eat in an hour, and when it was time I could join him. I accepted his offer and slept soundly for an hour. Then we went over to the officers' mess, where I took off my jacket and had the luck to find I was wearing my *Pour le mérite*. But, unfortunately, I was not wearing a uniform jacket, only a vest. I asked to be excused because I was not better dressed. Suddenly my good host discovered my *Pour le mérite*. He was speechless with astonishment and assured me that he did not know who I was. I told him my name once more. Now it seemed to dawn on him that he had indeed heard of me before. I now received oysters and champagne and had a splendid time, until Karl Schäfer came with my car to fetch me. From him I learned the name of the pilot of the other fallen Albatros. Lübbert had again done honor to his nickname. He was called "Bullet Catcher" because his machine suffered badly in every battle.

Once he showed sixty-four hits, without having been wounded himself. This time he had been grazed along the chest and lay in the field hospital. I flew his machine back to the field. Unfortunately, this outstanding officer, who had the stuff to one day become a Boelcke, died a hero's death for the fatherland some weeks later.

In the evening I was able to inform my host at Hénin-Liétard that I had increased my score to twenty-five that day.

A Flier's Trick

(END OF MARCH 1917)

The name "Siegfried Line" is known to every youth in the German Republic. During the days in which we drew back from this position there was, of course, brisk activity in the air. While the enemy had already occupied our abandoned territory on the ground, we did not relinquish the air to the Englishmen. *Jagdstaffel Boelcke* took care of that. Only very cautiously did the Englishmen dare to come out of their position type of warfare into the air.

That was the time when our dear Prince Friedrich Karl gave his life for the fatherland.

During a pursuit flight with *Jagdstaffel Boelcke, Leutnant* Werner Voss[17] was victorious in aerial combat with an Englishman. He had forced him to land in neutral territory between the lines. We had of course already abandoned this position, but the enemy had not yet occupied it. Only patrols,

[17] Voss, whom Arch Whitehouse described as "the son of a Jewish dyer from Krefeld," was a top ace who fought a most memorable battle, single-handedly, against an entire flight of the Royal Flying Corps, including the great James McCudden.

English as well as German, were in this unoccupied zone. The English airplane landed between the lines, and the Englishman probably believed that this territory had already been occupied by his own forces, an assumption in which he was justified. But Voss was of a different opinion. Shortly thereafter he decided to land near his victim. With great haste he loaded the enemy machine gun and other useful parts from the enemy's aircraft into his own. Then he lit a match to the enemy machine and in a few moments it went up in bright flames. A moment later, he was up in his victorious charger smilingly waving to the Englishmen then gathering on all sides below.

Hot Day

The second of April, 1917, was another hot day for my squadron. From our field we could hear the sounds of the bombardment, and it was certainly very heavy that day.

I was still in bed when the orderly rushed in crying: *"Herr Leutnant,* the English are here!" Still somewhat sleepy, I looked out the window and there circling over the field were my dear "friends." I got out of bed, quickly put my things on and got ready. My red bird was all set to begin the morning's work. My mechanics knew that I would not let this favorable moment go by without taking advantage of it. Everything was ready. I quickly donned my flight suit and was off.

Even so, I was last to start. My comrades got much closer to the enemy. Then, suddenly, one of the impudent fellows fell on me, attempting to force me down. I calmly let him come on, and then we began a merry dance. At one point my opponent flew on his back, then he did this, then that. It was a two-seater. I was superior to him, and he soon realized that he could not escape me. During a pause in the fighting

I looked around and saw that we were alone. Therefore, who-ever shot better, whoever had the greatest calm and the best position in the moment of danger, would win.

It did not take long. I squeezed under him and fired, but without causing serious damage. We were at least two kilo-meters from the Front and I thought he would land, but I miscalculated my opponent. When only a few meters above the ground, he suddenly leveled off and flew straight ahead, seeking to escape me. That was too bad for him. I attacked him again and went so low that I feared I would touch the houses in the village beneath me. The Englishman kept fighting back. Almost at the end I felt a hit on my machine. I must not let up now; he must fall. He crashed at full speed into a block of houses, and there was not much left. It was again a case of splendid daring. He defended himself right up to the end.

Very pleased with the results of my red "bicycle" in the morning's work, I turned back. My comrades were still in the air and were very surprised when, as we later sat down to breakfast, I told them of my number thirty-two. A very young lieutenant had shot down his first, and we were all happy.

I then made up for the morning ablutions I had missed. Later, a good friend—*Leutnant* Voss of *Jagdstaffel Boelcke*—came to visit me, and we had a long and delightful conversa-tion. The day before, Voss had scored his twenty-third victory. Therefore, he ranked next to me and was indeed, at the time, my most vigorous competition.

As he flew home I accompanied him part of the way. We went a roundabout way over the Front. The weather became so very bad we gave up hope of finding more game.

Beneath us were dense clouds. Voss, who did not know the area, was beginning to get uncomfortable. Over Arras I met my brother, who is also in my squadron, and who had gotten lost from his group. He joined us when he recognized my red bird.

Then we saw an enemy squadron approaching from the other side. Immediately, "Number thirty-three!" flashed through my head. However, the nine Englishmen were over their own territory and they preferred to avoid battle. (I will change the color of my plane the next time!) But we caught them. Fast machines are the important factors in combat.

I was closest to the enemy and attacked the one farthest back. To my great delight, he also wanted to engage me in battle. Looking around, I was pleased to see he had been deserted by his comrades and I was soon alone with him. He was the same type I had fought with in the morning. He knew what it was all about and was a very good shot. I found that out very well, to my sorrow. The favorable wind came to my aid and carried us both over the German lines. My opponent realized that the situation was not to his advantage and disappeared in a dive into a cloud. It was almost his salvation. I dived after him, came out below and miraculously found myself sitting behind him. I fired, and fired, but there was no tangible result. Then—finally I hit him. I noticed it from the white vapor of fuel he left behind. Consequently, his engine stopped and he had to land.

But he was a stubborn fellow. He must have recognized that he had played to the end. If he continued to shoot, I could immediately shoot him dead, for we were only three hundred meters up. But this fellow defended himself, exactly as the fellow in the morning had, until he landed. After his landing I flew over him again at ten meters altitude in order to determine whether or not I had killed him. What did the impertinent fellow do? He took his machine gun and shot up my whole machine.

Voss said to me afterwards, if that had happened to him, he would have flown back and shot him dead on the ground. This fellow was, indeed, one of the few lucky ones who remained alive.

Very pleased, I flew home and celebrated my thirty-third.

1   Rittmeister Manfred Freiherr von Richthofen *(National Archives)*

2 The Baron and his famous Jagdstaffel 11 (*United States Air Force*)

3 (*Left*) Von Richthofen suiting up to go aloft in his Albatros (*Peter Kilduff*)

4 (*Right*) Von Richthofen making last-minute adjustments to his flight suit prior to taking off in his Albatros D V from a naval air station (*National Archives*)

5 *(Above)* Von Richthofen speaking with a fellow officer in front of his famous all-red Fokker triplane *(National Archives)* 6 *(Left)* Captain A. Roy Brown, the Canadian flier credited with shooting down the Red Baron *(Royal Canadian Air Force)*

7 Oberleutnant Max Immelmann
(National Archives)

8 Werner Voss and his motorcycle
(National Archives)

9 Oberleutnant Ernst Udet
(*National Archives*)

10 Ernst Udet (*left*), Bruno Loerzer
(*right*) and their friend, Siegmund Abel
(*rear*) (*National Archives*)

11 Lothar von Richthofen, younger brother of the Red Baron, and his Fokker D VII *(National Archives)*

12 Hermann Göring in the cockpit of his Fokker triplane *(National Archives)*

13 "Fat Hermann" during later, inglorious Nazi times *(National Archives)*

14 Kaiser Wilhelm (*National Archives*)

15 General Erich Ludendorff, chief of staff to Field Marshal Paul von Hindenburg (*National Archives*) **16** Field Marshal Paul von Hindenburg, victor over the Russians at Tannenberg, supreme commander of the Central Powers forces, and later President of the German Republic (*National Archives*)

17 The *Pour le Mérite* or "Blue Max" *(Twentieth Century-Fox)*

18 Albatros C III two-seater in flight *(National Archives)*

Le diable rouge

The weather was marvelous as we stood on the field. I had just had a visit from a gentleman who had never seen an air fight or anything similar and assured me that he was enormously interested in seeing such an air battle.

We climbed into our crates, laughing at him, Schäfer suggested: "We could have fun with him!" So we placed him before a telescope and flew away.

The day began well. We had scarcely reached two thousand meters when the first Englishman in a squadron of five came at us. After the attack, which was similar to a cavalry charge, the enemy squadron lay demolished on the ground. Not a single one of us was even wounded. The opposition went down on our side of the lines—two in flames.

My good friend down on the ground was more than a little amazed. He had imagined the matter quite differently, much more dramatically. He thought the whole affair looked quite harmless until suddenly some of the airplanes plunged down, burning like rockets. I have gradually become accustomed to the view, but I must say I had a similar reaction witnessing my first aerial death, and I have long since had nightmares of the first Englishman I saw plummeting down. I believe if it happened to me again it would not be so terrible as it was that first time.

With the day begun so well, we sat ourselves down to a decent breakfast, as we were all ravenously hungry. Meanwhile, our airplanes were brought out again and reloaded with ammunition for our next flight.

In the evening we forwarded the proud report to Headquarters: "Thirteen enemy airplanes destroyed by six German machines."

Jagdstaffel Boelcke was able to make such a high-scoring report only one more time. That time we shot down eight machines. This day we had brought down four machines more.[18] It was mainly done by *Leutnant* Wolff, a delicate, slender little fellow whom one would never expect to have been such a great victor. My brother got two, Schäfer got two, Sebastian Festner got two, and I got three. We went to bed that evening tremendously proud but quite tired.

The next day we read with great exultation the Army Report of our deeds of the day before. One of the Englishmen we had shot down was taken prisoner, and we went over to talk to him. He, too, inquired about the red machine. It was not unknown to the troops in the trenches, who called it *"Le diable rouge."* The rumor had spread in his squadron that a girl piloted the red machine, somewhat like Joan of Arc. He was very surprised when I assured him that the alleged "girl" stood before him at the time. He was not trying to make a joke; rather, he was convinced that only a maiden could actually sit in the garishly painted crate.

"Moritz"

The most beautiful creature ever created is my elm-colored Great Dane, my "little lap dog"—Moritz. I bought him for five Marks from a nice Belgian in Ostend. The mother was a beautiful animal, as was his sire; he was therefore quite purebred. I am convinced of that. Zeumer took a second one and called him "Max." Max came to a sudden end under an automobile, but Moritz thrived splendidly. He slept in bed with me and was very well trained. Ever since Ostend he had accompanied me step by step and has grown in my heart.

---

[18] Von Richthofen's arithmetic is in error.

From month to month Moritz got bigger and bigger, and gradually my tender little lap dog developed into quite an enormous animal.

I even took him up with me once. He had become my "leading observer." He behaved very sensibly and eyed the world with interest from above. However, my mechanics were angry afterwards because they had to clean the airplane of some unpleasant things. But Moritz was very pleased by it all.

He is now more than a year old, but still a puppy. He plays billiards very well. Unfortunately, many balls, and particularly many billiard cloths, have long since gone by the way. He also has quite an instinct for hunting. My mechanics are very happy about this, for he has brought them many nice hares. But he gets a good thrashing from me for it, as I am little pleased by this passion.

He has one stupid trait. He loved to accompany the airplanes as they start down the field. Many a flier's dog, while doing this, has been killed by a propeller. Once Moritz chased after a starting airplane, and caught it, unfortunately—and a very beautiful propeller was ruined. Moritz howled terribly, but one of my training failures was made up for in this way. I had always resisted having him clipped, that is, having his ears specially cut. Now the propeller had made up for it on one side. Vanity never bothered him, but the one floppy ear and the other half-clipped do not go well together. In general, if he did not have that defect he would be a handsome hound.

Moritz understood the World War and our enemies very well. When, in the summer of 1916, he saw Russian natives for the first time—the train had stopped and Moritz was being taken for a walk—he chased after the fleeing Russian youths amid an enormous clatter. He also did not care for Frenchmen, although he himself was really a Belgian. I once left orders with the servants in some new quarters to clean the house. When I came home in the evening, nothing had

been done. Angrily I ordered one of the servants, a Frenchman, to come to me. Scarcely had he opened the door when
Moritz greeted him somewhat unfriendlily. Now I could
account for why the gentleman had avoided cleaning my
château.

English Bombing Attack on the Airfield

Nights when the moon is full are the most suitable for
night flights. During the full-moon nights of April 1917, our
English "friends" were particularly active in conjunction with
the battle of Arras. They probably found out that we had set
ourselves up quite comfortably at a very nice large airfield in
Douai.

One night as we sat in the officers' mess, the telephone
rang and it was announced: "The English are coming." Naturally there was a great hullabaloo of activity. We already
had shelters; Simon, our construction boss, had seen to that.
Everyone dived into the shelters and then we heard, faintly
at first, the noise of an airplane engine. The flak and search-
light batteries appeared to have gotten the announcement
when we did, for we noticed that they came to life slowly.
However, the first enemy aircraft was much too far away to
be attacked. We had a grand time. We only feared that the
Englishmen would not find our field, for it was not at all
simple at night, especially since we did not lie alongside a
road, or near water, or near a railway line, which would make
the best reference points at night.

Apparently the Englishmen flew very high. First they went
once entirely around the field—we thought they were looking
for another target—then suddenly one of them switched his
engine off and came diving down. "Now it is getting serious,"
Wolff said. We each had a carbine and began to shoot at the

Englishman. We could not even see him yet, but the noise of our shooting calmed our nerves. Then he came into the search-light. All over the airfield there was great commotion. It was quite an old crate which we recognized immediately. He was, at most, a kilometer away from us. He flew right toward our field, coming ever closer. When he was at about a hundred-meter altitude he switched the engine on again and flew right over us. Wolff said: "Thank God, he was looking at the other side of the airfield." But it did not take long for the first, and then other, bombs to rain down. Our "friend" put on a won-derful fireworks display, which could only impress a scared rabbit. I find, in general, bombing at night has only a moral significance. If one fills his pants, it is very uncomfortable or embarrassing; but it is seldom more harmful than this.

We made a great joke of this and hoped that the English would come often. Consequently, the "lattice-tail"[19] dropped his bombs from a fifty-meter altitude, and flew safely away which is somewhat impertinent, for I'm sure with a full moon, I would not miss a shot at a wild boar from fifty meters. Why couldn't I hit an Englishman? It would be something to shoot down one of these "friends" from the ground. We often had that honor in the air, but I had not tried it from the ground. When the Englishmen left, we went back into the mess and promised we would prepare a better reception for them the next night.

The next day the orderlies and other enlisted men busied themselves near the mess and the officers' living quarters, driving in poles which in the coming night would be used as machine-gun stands. We adjusted the range on several cap-tured English airplane machine guns for night shooting and were very excited about what would happen. I will not reveal the number of machine guns, but it was enough. Each of my gentlemen was armed with one.

[19] German description of certain two-seat "pusher" aircraft

That night we again sat in the mess, naturally talking about night fliers, when an orderly burst in and cried: "They are coming, they are coming!" Finishing his announcement, he disappeared, somewhat sparsely dressed, into the next shelter. Each of us rushed to a machine gun. Some of the qualified enlisted marksmen were also armed with machine guns. Everyone else had carbines. In any case, the squadron was armed to the teeth and ready to receive the English gentlemen.

The first came, just as on the evening before, at great altitude, then down to fifty meters and, to our great joy, he aimed this time at the site of our barracks. He was caught in the searchlight no more than three hundred meters away from us. The first of our men began to shoot, and we all joined in at the same time. An infantry assault charge could not have been better repelled. This poor fellow was greeted by furious ground fire which he could not have heard over the noise of his engine, but he would see the flashes of our gunfire. I thought it very plucky of him that he did not swerve but stubbornly continued on his mission. He flew right over us. The moment he was above us, we of course all jumped into a shelter, for to be hit by a stupid bomb would be a foolish hero's death for a fighter pilot. Scarcely had he passed over us when we were back at our guns, firing after him. Schäfer claimed, of course: "I hit him!" Schäfer shoots well, but in this case I did not believe him, and, besides, everyone else had just as good a chance of hitting the Englishman.

If nothing else, the enemy was forced to drop his bombs in the area without effect. One landed a few meters from *"Le petit rouge,"* but did not harm it. Later that night this fun was repeated. I was already in bed and fast asleep when, as if in a dream, I heard antiaircraft fire. I woke up only to learn that the dream was really happening. One fellow flew so low over my room that I pulled the covers over my head in fright. The next minute there was a terrific noise near my window, and the panes of glass fell victim to the bomb. Quickly I jumped into my shirt in order to get a few shots at him. Outside he was the target of vigorous shooting. Unfortunately, I had outslept my comrades.

The next morning we were pleasantly surprised to learn that we had brought down no less than three Englishmen. They landed not far from our airfield and were taken prisoner. We had hit their engines and thereby forced them down on our side. So, perhaps Schäfer had not been mistaken, after all. In any event, we were very pleased with our success. The Englishmen were somewhat less pleased, however, and they preferred not to attack our field anymore.

Schäfer's Forced Landing Behind the Lines

On the evening of April 22, 1917, we made a pursuit flight and came home very late, losing Emil Schäfer along the way. Of course, everyone hoped he would reach the field before darkness. Nine o'clock came and then ten o'clock, and Schäfer still had not returned. He could not have had any more fuel, so he must have made a forced landing somewhere. No one was willing to admit that he had been shot down. No one dared say it, but everyone feared it silently. The front-line telephone network was set in motion to determine where a flier had landed. No one could give us any information. No division, no brigade had seen him. This was an unpleasant situation. We went to bed expressing the firm conviction that he would be found. At two o'clock in the morning I was suddenly awakened. The telephone orderly informed me, beaming: "Schäfer is in Sailly and asks to be fetched."

The next morning at breakfast the door opened and my good friend stood before me in clothes as filthy as if he had been among the corpses of the battle of Arras for two weeks. A great commotion arose. Schäfer was very happy and had to tell his experiences. He was hungry as a bear, so after he had eaten breakfast he told us the following story:

"I was flying home along the Front when I saw what was apparently an enemy ground-support aircraft at quite low altitude. I attacked him and shot him down. I was preparing to fly back when the Englishmen in the trenches below made up their minds to pepper me. My salvation, of course, was the speed of the airplane, for in shooting, the fellows did not of course think to shoot in front of me. I was perhaps two hundred meters up. Suddenly there was a loud noise and my engine stopped. I had to land. The question was, Would I get over the enemy lines or not? The Englishmen noticed I was hit and began to shoot frantically. Now I heard every single shot, for the engine no longer ran and the propeller stood still. It was a painful situation. I landed, and my machine had not even stopped when tremendous machine-gun fire came from a hedge near the village of Monchy near Arras. The bullets pounded my machine. I jumped out of the crate and dove into the nearest shell hole. There I gave some thought about where I was. Gradually it became clear to me that I was on the other side of the lines and damned close to the enemy. Thank God it was late in the evening. That was my salvation.

"It was not long before the first shells came. Of course they were gas bombs and, obviously, I did not have a gas mask with me, so my eyes began to water terribly. Before darkness the Englishmen trained their machine guns on my landing place; some were quite obviously aimed at my airplane, others at my shell crater. The bullets splashed above me. I tried to calm my nerves and lit a cigarette. Then I took off my thick fur jacket, made a leap out of the shell hole, and ran for my life! Each minute seemed like an hour.

"Gradually it grew darker. I heard partridges clucking around me. As a hunter I knew these birds were quite peaceful and friendly; consequently, there was no danger of being surprised in my hiding place. After dark a pair of partridges near me suddenly flew up, then a second pair, and I knew something was wrong. Evidently it was a patrol looking for me. Now it was high time for me to take off. Quite carefully at first I crept on my belly from shell hole to shell hole. After an hour and a half of zealous creeping I came to the first humans. Were they Englishmen or were they Germans? They approached, and as they came near I could have hugged them when I recognized them as our own musketeers on patrol in no-man's-land. One of the men led me to his company commander, and there I learned that earlier in the evening I had landed about fifty paces from the enemy lines and that our infantry had already given me up for lost. First I had a decent supper, and then I set out on the march back.

"There was more shooting behind me than in front of me. Every path, every trench, every bush, every gorge, all lay under enemy fire. The English were scheduled to attack the next morning; therefore, they must have begun their artillery preparation that evening. I had chosen an unfavorable day for my escape attempt. At two o'clock in the morning I reached a telephone and reported to the squadron."

We were all happy to have our Schäfer with us again. He went to bed. Any other man would have renounced the pleasure of pursuit flying for the next day or so, but on the afternoon of the same day my friend Schäfer attacked a low-flying B.E. over Monchy.

The Anti-Richthofen Squadron

The English devised a fine scheme to either capture or shoot me down. For this purpose they had actually set up a special squadron that patrolled our area. We discovered this when it was noted that their attacks were mainly directed against our red airplanes.

I must point out that we had the whole *Jagdstaffel* painted red, for it had gradually become clear to our "friends" that I sat in a glaring red crate. When we were all painted red, the Englishmen were astonished, for instead of one they saw a dozen such crates. But that did not keep them from making an attempt to attack us. I much prefer to have my customers come to me than to have to go to them.

We flew up to the Front in hope of finding the enemy. After about twenty minutes the first ones arrived and really pounced on us. That had not happened to us for a long time. The English had somewhat curtailed their famous offensive spirit, for it had indeed gotten too costly for them. There were three Englishmen in Spad[20] single-seaters who believed themselves to be very superior to us because of their good machines.

Wolff, my brother and I flew together. Three against three—that was just as it should be. Right at the beginning their attack became defensive. However, we soon had the upper hand. I selected my opponent, and I could quickly see that my brother and Wolff had each engaged one. The usual dance began, each circling the other. A favorable wind came to our aid. It carried the combatants away from the Front, toward Germany.

My opponent was the first to fall, after I had shot his engine to pieces. In any case, he decided to land near us. I no longer knew clemency, so I attacked him a second time, whereupon the airplane fell apart in my stream of bullets. The wings fell separately like pieces of paper, and the fuselage dropped like a burning stone. The pilot fell into a marsh. We could not dig him out. I never learned my opponent's identity. He simply disappeared. Only the last remains of the tail burned and marked the spot where he had dug his own grave.

[20] Spad VII

At the same time Wolff and my brother had attacked their opponents and forced them to land not far from mine.

We flew home very pleased and thought: "Hopefully, the Anti-Richthofen Squadron will come often."

The "Old Master" Comes to Visit Us

My father announced one day that he wanted to visit his two sons. My father is the local commandant of a small town in the vicinity of Lille and, consequently, was not far from us. I could often see him from above. He arrived by train at nine o'clock, and by nine-thirty was at our field. We had just come home from a pursuit flight and my brother was first to jump out of his crate and greet the "old master": "Hello, Papa, I have just shot down an Englishman." After which I jumped out of my machine and said: "Hello, Papa, I have just shot down an Englishman." The old gentleman was very happy; one could see that he thought that flying was great fun. He was not afraid for his sons; on the contrary, he would just as soon have gotten in the machine and shot down an Englishman himself—at least I believe that. We had breakfast with him first, then we flew on patrol again.

In the meantime an air fight took place over our new airfield. My father observed this with great interest. We were not involved, for we were standing below and watching it ourselves. The fight involved an English squadron which had broken through our defences and was being attacked by some of our reconnaissance aircraft over our airfield. Suddenly one airplane flipped over, recovered itself again and came down in a normal glide; we recognized with regret that this one was a German. The Englishmen flew away. The German airplane had apparently been shot up, but it was making its descent under control. The pilot attempted to land at our airfield, which was rather small for such a big airplane. The ground was unfamiliar to the pilot, so the landing was anything but smooth. We ran toward the wreckage, where we noted with regret that one of the crew, the machine gunner, had been killed. This sight was somewhat new to my father, and it obviously made him more serious.

The day promised to be a good one for us. The weather was wonderfully clear. The antiaircraft guns could be heard constantly, so obviously there was considerable flying activity. Toward midday we went up again. This time I once again was lucky and shot down my second Englishman of the day. After dinner I took a short nap and awoke in tiptop condition. At this time Wolff was off fighting with his group and got one himself, as did Schäfer.

That afternoon my brother and I started out twice more with Schäfer, Festner and Allmenröder. The first flight was unsuccessful, the second flight much better. We were not at the Front long when an enemy squadron came toward us. Unfortunately, they were higher than we were and we could do nothing. We tried to reach their altitude but failed. We had to let them go and continued flying along over the Front; my brother was close by me, in front of the others. Then I saw two enemy artillery observation aircraft coming near our Front. I signaled my brother and he understood. We flew close together, increasing our speed. We each felt superior to the enemy and, more than anything else, knew that we could rely on each other. That is the main point; one must know with whom one flies. My brother was first to approach the enemy, attacking the first one to fly near him, and I went after the second.

I looked around quickly to make sure a third was not in the vicinity, but we were alone: eye to eye. I soon got on the favorable side of my opponent, fired a short burst, and the enemy airplane exploded. I had never had a battle end so quickly.

While I observed where the debris of my opponent was falling, I looked at my brother. He was scarcely five hundred meters away from me and right in the midst of battle with his opponent.

Watching this scene, I must say, I could not have done better myself. Lothar had taken the opponent by surprise and had circled behind him. Then suddenly the enemy airplane reared up—a sure sign of being hit. Lothar had no doubt shot the pilot in the head. The airplane dived and its wings came off one after the other. The wreckage fell in the vicinity of my victim. I flew near my brother and waved congratulations to him. We were satisfied and flew off. It is nice when one can fly with one's brother.

Our comrades, meanwhile, had flown nearby and watched the drama that we offered them. They could not help, as one should only shoot when he is busy with an opponent; the others could only watch and cover our back, so that we were not attacked by a third from behind.

We flew on, climbing to a higher altitude, for some of the Anti-Richthofen Club were up above. We were easy to recognize; the sun from the west illuminated our machines and showed our beautiful red color from far away. We drew tightly together, for each of us knew that our "friends" followed the same calling we did. Unfortunately, they were higher, so we had to wait for their attack. The famous triplanes[21] and Spads were completely new machines, but the crate does not matter as much as who sits in it. Our "friends" were cautious and had no spunk. We offered to fight them here on our side or over on theirs. But they would not accept. Why do they first show off when in squadron formation, and then later, when near us, let their hearts fall into their shoes?

One of them finally got his courage up and dropped down on our man in the rear. Of course the challenge was accepted,

21 Sopwith triplanes

even though it was unfavorable for us; for he who is on the attack side has the advantage. But if one of the customers no longer pays attention to his business, I think one must take what comes along. Therefore, everyone turned around. The Englishman noticed this and immediately broke off. But a beginning had been made. Another Englishman tried the same thing. He had sought me as an opponent, and I greeted him with a salvo from both machine guns. He did not seem to appreciate this and tried to escape me by diving away. That was his undoing. Now I was above him. Whatever is beneath me, alone and over our territory where possible, is indeed as good as lost, especially if it is a single-seater, a fighter plane which cannot shoot from the rear. The opponent had a very good machine and was very fast, but it was not his luck to reach his lines. Over Lens I began to fire at him. I was too far away. But that was a trick of mine; I upset him that way. He fell into the trap and made banking turns. I used this as an opportunity to get closer. Quickly I tried the same maneuver again and a third time. My "friend" tried unsuccessfully to escape. Thus, my shots gradually approached him. Now I was quite close—at the most, fifty meters away from him. I took aim, waited a moment, then pushed the buttons of both machine guns. First there was a faint trail of smoke, the sure sign of a hit in the fuel tank, then a bright flame, and he disappeared below.

This was my fourth of the day. My brother got two. Apparently we had invited the old gentleman to a feast. Our joy was boundless.

In the evening I invited some gentlemen over, among whom was my good friend Wedel, who by chance was in the area. It was all a most successful and enjoyable affair.

Both brothers had shot down six Englishmen in one day. That is a whole squadron. I believe the English were unsympathetic toward us.

Flight Home

Then I reached a total of fifty enemy aircraft shot down. I would have preferred fifty-two; therefore, I shot down two more the same day, although that was really against orders.

Strictly speaking, I had been allowed only forty-one; why the number forty-one was decreed is anyone's guess, but I tried to ignore it. I am no record-keeper. In the Flying Service records are far from our thoughts. One only fulfills one's duty. Boelcke would have shot down a hundred if he had not had the fatal accident. And many another of our good fallen comrades would have achieved higher numbers if their sudden deaths had not prevented it. But it is still fun to have gotten half a hundred. Now I had finally reached the fifty I had been allowed before being sent on leave.

In the evening of the same day the telephone rang, and nothing short of "Supreme Headquarters" wished to speak with me. It seemed to be the greatest fun to be connected with the "great office." Among other things I received the delightful news that His Majesty had expressed the wish to speak with me personally and specifically set the day to be the second of May. But this reached me at nine o'clock of the thirtieth of April. It would not have been possible to go by train to comply with the wish of the all-high warlord, so I decided to make the trip by air, which is indeed more desirable. The next morning I started out, not in my single-seater, *Le petit rouge,* but in a big fat two-seater.

I sat in the rear instead of at the controls. In this case the piloting was done by *Leutnant* Krefft, one of the gentlemen of my squadron. He was going on sick leave, therefore it worked out wonderfully well. He would arrive home even quicker, an idea not at all disagreeable to him.

My departure was head over heels. I could take nothing more than a toothbrush with me in the airplane, therefore I had to appear at Supreme Headquarters dressed as I was. And a soldier does not have many beautiful items of clothing in the field; in any event, not a poor Front hog like myself.

My brother took over command of the squadron. I briefly said goodby, for I hoped soon to return to take up my duties again in the company of these fine fellows.

The flight went over Lüttich, Namur, Aachen and Cologne. It was beautiful to sail through the sea of air without war-like thoughts. The weather was splendid. We had not had such clear skies for a long time. Certainly there would have been much to do at the Front these days. Soon even our observation balloons were out of sight. The thunder of the battle of Arras lay even further back. Beneath us was a picture of peace: steamers sailing on the rivers, and an express train, which we easily overtook, whistling through the country-side. The wind was in our favor. The earth appeared as flat as a barn door. The beautiful mountains of the Meuse did not even look like mountains; one could not even recognize them by their shadows because they were perpendicular to us. One only knew they were there and, with a little imagination, one could hide in their cool ravines.

It was getting rather late, toward the dinner hour, as a cloud layer drew together beneath us and covered the earth fully. After orienting ourselves by the sun and the compass, we flew on. Gradually we came in the vicinity of neutral Holland, which was not good for us. So we decided to go down to determine our position. We went beneath the clouds and found ourselves directly over Namur. From there we went on to Aachen. We left Aachen on our left and at midday reached Cologne. Our spirits were raised. We had a long leave before us, not to mention the beautiful weather, the success of having gotten as far as Cologne, and the certainty that, de-spite whatever else happened, we would reach Supreme Headquarters.

Our arrival in Cologne had been announced by telegraph, so we were expected. My fifty-second aerial victory had appeared in the newspapers the day before, so the reception was held accordingly.

I had a headache from the three-hour flight, so I took a little midday nap before setting out for Supreme Headquarters. From Cologne we now flew part of the way along the Rhine. I knew the section. I had often traveled there by steamer, by car and by train. And now, by airplane. Which was the nicest? That is hard to say. Naturally, one sees certain details better from a steamer. But the over-all view from the airplane is also not to be scorned. The Rhine has a special charm, even from above. We did not fly too high, in order not to lose the feeling of the mountains, whose giant wooded heights are the most beautiful part of the Rhine. Of course, we could not see the individual houses. Too bad one cannot fly at both slow and fast speeds. I would certainly have set the flight at the slowest speed possible.

Only too quickly one beautiful picture after another disappeared. When one flies higher one does not have the feeling of going forward very fast. In a car or an express train, for example the speed appears tremendous, as opposed to an airplane, which really seems to be moving slowly when one has reached a certain altitude. One notices its speed when one had not looked out for five minutes and then suddenly tries to get oriented to the surroundings. The picture one had in mind shortly before is suddenly changed completely. What one saw beneath earlier is now seen at a different and strange angle. Therefore, one can quickly become disoriented if one fails to pay attention for a moment.

We arrived at Supreme Headquarters in the afternoon and were heartily received by some comrades I knew who worked in the "great office." I really felt sorry for these "pencil-pushers." They have only half the fun of war. Next I reported to the Commanding General of the Air Service.[22]

[22] General Von Hoeppner

The next morning the great moment came, and I was presented to Generals Von Hindenburg and Ludendorff. I had to wait quite a while, but first I reported to Von Hindenburg, then to Ludendorff.

It is a weird feeling to be in the room where the destiny of the world is decided, so I was quite happy when I left the "great office" behind me and, at midday, was commanded to have breakfast with His Majesty, the Emperor. It was my birthday. Someone must have disclosed this to His Majesty, and so he congratulated me—once for my success, then for the twenty-fifth year of my life. He also surprised me with a small birthday present.

I would never have dreamed that on my twenty-fifth birthday I would sit to the right of the Emperor and be mentioned in a speech of General Field Marshal Von Hindenburg.

The next day I was invited to dine with Her Majesty, the Empress, and so I traveled to Bad Homburg.[23] There I had breakfast with Her Majesty and was also given a birthday present. I had the great pleasure of demonstrating the start of a flight for Her Majesty. In the evening I was again invited to be with General Field Marshal Von Hindenburg.

The following day I flew to Freiburg to shoot wood grouse. From Freiburg I flew as a passenger to Berlin. We refueled in Nürnberg, as a thunderstorm was coming and I was in a great hurry to get to Berlin. All manner of more or less interesting things awaited me there, so we flew on despite the thunderstorm. I laughed at the clouds and the beastly weather even though the rain came down in buckets. Now and then there was hail. The propeller later looked absurd; beaten by hailstones, it looked like a saw blade. Unfortunately, the weather was so much fun for me that I completely lost track of my position. I tried to orient myself, but I did not have the haziest idea where I was. A nice mess! To have lost my

[23] A spa in southern Germany which was the favorite of European nobility

way at home! Of course that had to happen to me. How they would be amused at home if they knew. But the fact could not be helped; I no longer knew where I was. Due to the strong wind and low flying, I was driven off course. Using the sun and compass, I kept flying roughly in the direction of Berlin. Cities, villages, rivers and forests rushed beneath me, but I recognized nothing. I checked my map, but it was futile. Everything was different. As it later turned out, I had flown about a hundred kilometers off course. Actually, I was no longer on the map and it would not have been possible for me to recognize the area.

After a flight of about two hours, my copilot and I decided on a forced landing. That is always unpleasant, especially without an airfield. One does not know how the ground surface is. If a wheel goes into a hole, the crate is finished. First we tried to make out the name of a train station, but there was no hope of that. It was of course written so small that one could not make out a letter of it. Therefore, we had to land. We had heavy hearts, but there was nothing else to do. We sought a meadow that looked quite nice from above and tried our luck. Unfortunately, on closer inspection the meadow did not look too good. This I determined later from a slightly bent undercarriage. We had spattered ourselves in glory. First we had lost our way and then smashed up the crate. We had to make the rest of our journey home by quite ordinary locomotion, the express train. Slowly but surely we reached Berlin. We had made a forced landing in the vicinity of Leipzig. Had we not made the blunder, we would certainly have already arrived in Berlin, but sometimes no matter what one does, it is wrong.

A few days later I arrived in my hometown of Schweidnitz. Although it was seven o'clock in the morning, quite a crowd of people were waiting at the station. The welcome was hearty. In the afternoon different honors were accorded me, even one by the Boy Scouts.

On the whole, it became clear to me that the hometown is vividly interested in its soldiers in the field.

I read in *Der Vossischer Zeitung:*
"The English have put together a squadron of volunteer fliers whose exclusive aim is the destruction of the most successful German fighter pilot *Rittmeister*[24] *Freiherr*[25] Von Richthofen, who has already shot down fifty-two enemy fliers. The pilot who succeeds in shooting down or capturing Von Richthofen will receive the Victoria Cross, a promotion, his own airplane as a gift, 5000 pounds sterling, and a special prize from the aircraft factory whose airplane the pilot uses. Flying with the English squadron will be a motion-picture cameraman who will record the whole event for the purpose of later utilization in a British Army film."

This is a great honor for me, but I must honestly say that it also turns out to be a great embarrassment. If we accept this, the following could take place:

Suppose it is Sunday. I lie in bed, dozing. My orderly rushes in and yells: *"Herr Rittmeister,* the English Anti-Richthofen Squadron challenges you!" There remains nothing else for me to do but to spring from my bed, jump into my crate and be off into the sky. Consequently, I am now in the air and the business begins . . . I will not overdo it, because I have the sinister feeling that the Englishmen are not going to settle the business with me quite according to plan, as they had imagined. For, by way of example, what happens if I look around and fire and am so unlucky as to shoot the cameraman! What then? The entire British Army will be inconvenienced and the film ruined. The "gentlemen" on the other side will be in serious difficulty and will blame it all on me, of course.

How would these "gentlemen" behave if a number of other

[24] Cavalry Captain, Von Richthofen's actual rank
[25] Title of nobility denoting a rank slightly below a baron with no English equivalent—considered as a baron, however

"gentlemen" went up in order to shoot them down and were filmed being shot down by them? I believe the heart of the matter is to first shoot down the cameraman!

But how is it when the situation is reversed? How is it if I shoot down the English squadron? Do I receive the Victoria Cross, a promotion, my own airplane as a present, 5000 pounds sterling, and a special prize from the aircraft factory whose airplane I use?

But I am satisfied. I only want to get the cameraman who is supposed to film me when I am shot down. That I want very much!

My Brother

I had not been on leave eight days when I received this message: "Lothar is wounded, but not mortally." No more. Direct inquiries revealed that he had been on a flight with Allmenröder against the enemy. Then he saw beneath him, somewhat far over the other side, an Englishman buzzing around alone. It was one of the enemy infantry spotters who are such a nuisance to our troops. It is questionable whether they really achieve anything with their crawling around. In any case, they are a nuisance. My brother was about two thousand meters up; the Englishman, a thousand. Lothar stalked him, went into a dive and was on him in a few seconds. The Englishman decided to avoid battle and likewise disappeared down below in a dive. My brother, without hesitating, went after him. He did not care if it was on their side or ours. He had only one thought: The enemy must go down. If my brother does not get at least one victory on every flight, the whole enterprise is no fun for him. My brother caught up with him just above the ground and shot him full of holes. The Englishman plunged straight into the ground. There was nothing more to it.

After such a battle, especially at low altitude, in which one twists and turns, circling right and left, the average flier often has no idea where he is. Now on this day it was somewhat misty and, as a result, there was unfavorable weather. Quickly Lothar oriented himself and noticed he was quite a distance behind the Front. He was behind the Vimy heights, which are about a hundred meters higher than the surrounding area. In any case, my brother had disappeared behind these Vimy heights, according to the ground observers.

The flight home, until one reaches his own position, is not among the most comfortable feelings. One can do nothing in return if the enemy shoots at him. Only seldom do they hit, however. At such a low altitude one can hear every shot; it sounds like chestnuts popping in a fire when individual infantrymen shoot. As he neared the lines, he suddenly felt a knock. Hit! That was clear to him. He is one of those who cannot stand to see his own blood. Someone else's would make no impression on him. But his own blood upsets him. He felt something warm running down his right leg and at the same time a pain in his hip as well. Below, the shooting continued. Consequently, he was still on the other side. At last the shooting gradually stopped and he crossed over our Front. But now he had to hurry, for his strength was obviously leaving him. Then he saw a forest and, near it, a meadow. It had to be the meadow. The ignition was quickly shut off and the engine stopped; at the same moment he lost consciousness. Now he sat completely alone in his airplane; there was no one else to help him. How he came to earth is really a miracle. For no airplane starts and lands by itself. People maintain there is an old *"Taube"*[26] in Cologne that starts without a mechanic the moment a pilot sits in it, flies away by itself, makes curves and lands again after five minutes. Many men are said to have seen it. I have not seen it—but I

[26] Early German aircraft whose name would be translated as "Dove"

am firmly convinced it is true. In any event, my brother did not have such a *Taube* that landed by itself, but nevertheless, nothing happened to him when he made contact with the ground. He regained consciousness again in a field hospital. He was then transported to Douai.

It is quite a peculiar feeling for one brother to see another brother engaged in battle with an Englishman. I once saw, for example, how Lothar was attacked by an Englishman as he lagged behind the squadron. It would have been easy for him to avoid the battle. He had only to disappear down below. But no, he did not do that. Apparently the thought had not even occurred to him. He does not know how to run away. Luckily, I had observed this and was on the alert. Then I saw the Englishman who was above pounce on him and shoot. My brother tried to reach his altitude, with no concern of being shot at or not. Then suddenly his airplane looped and the red machine plunged straight down, spinning all the while. Not an expected movement, but a regular fall. This is not the nicest of all feelings for the watching brother. But I had to get used to it, for my brother used this trick. When he recognized that the Englishman was superior to him, he simulated being shot down. The Englishman went after him, but my brother started up again and in a twinkling he was above him. The enemy airplane could not come around as quickly to recover itself, and my brother was on his neck at once. Some moments later flames licked out from the enemy. Then there was nothing more to save—the airplane plunged down burning.

Once I stood near a fuel tank where a hundred liters had exploded and burned. I could not stand within ten paces of it, it was so hot. And now one must imagine a tank a few centimeters forward with fifty liters exploding and the blast from the propeller carrying the heat right into your face. I believe one loses consciousness in the first moment. In any case, this death is quickest.

But now and then a miracle happens. For example, I once saw an English airplane plunge down burning. The flames burst out first at an altitude of five hundred meters. The machine was wrapped in bright flames. When we flew home we learned that one of the crew had jumped out at fifty meters. It was the observer. Fifty meters altitude! One must think about the altitude. An average Berlin church tower is not much higher. If one should jump from the tip of such a tower! What would he be when he hit! Most people would break their necks jumping from the first floor. In any case, this brave observer jumped out of his burning airplane, which had already been burning for at least a minute, at fifty meters altitude and suffered nothing more than a fractured ankle. Right after this happened, he even made a statement that his morale had not suffered at all.

Another time I shot down an Englishman and the pilot had a fatal head wound. The airplane plunged straight down to earth from three thousand meters without starting again. Quite a while later I glided past there and saw nothing more than a deserted heap. To my astonishment, I learned that the observer had only a skull fracture and his condition was not serious. One must be lucky.

Another time Boelcke shot down a Nieuport. I saw it myself. The airplane dropped like a stone. We drove over there and found the airplane half buried in the loamy soil. The occupant, a fighter pilot, was unconscious from a stomach wound and had wrenched his arm on hitting. But he did not die.

On the other hand, I was a witness when a good friend of mine caught a wheel in a rabbit hole on landing. The machine had lost speed and went slowly up on its nose, pondering which side to tip on, then fell on its back—and the poor fellow inside broke his neck.

My brother Lothar is a lieutenant with the 4th Dragoons, attended the Military Academy before the war, was made an officer at the outbreak of war, and began the war as I did, as a cavalryman. What heroic deeds he has accomplished are unknown to me, as he never talks about himself. Only the following story has been told to me:

It was in the winter of 1914. His regiment lay on one side of the Warthe, the Russians on the other side. No one knew if they would move back or stay there. Part of the stream was frozen, so that it was difficult to ride through. There were, of course, no bridges, as the Russians had torn them down. Then my brother swam across, determined where the Russians were and swam back. This was all during the severe Russian winter when it was many degrees below zero. After a few minutes his clothes were frozen stiff, but he maintained that underneath he felt quite warm. He rode the whole day dressed this way until he returned to his quarters. He did not even catch cold from all this.

In the winter of 1915 he followed my advice and became an observer, as I had. Just a year later he was a pilot. He found, as had I, that the training to be an observer certainly is not difficult; nor is it to be a fighter pilot. In March 1917 he passed his third examination and was immediately assigned to my *Jagdstaffel*.

He was then a very young and cautious pilot who never thought of looping or such tricks, but was satisfied when he started a flight and landed in good order. Two weeks later I took him with me for the first time against the enemy and had him fly close behind me in order to observe what we did on such flights. After the third flight with him I suddenly saw him break away from me and jump on an Englishman and kill him. My heart leapt with joy as I watched this. It was again proof of how little art there is in shooting down an enemy. It is only the personality or, among other things, the energy of the one concerned that does the job. I am no Pégoud[27] and do not want to be one, I am only a soldier doing my duty. Four weeks later my brother had already shot down twenty Englishmen. A pilot who shoots down his first enemy two weeks after passing his third examination, and four weeks later has gotten twenty, must be unique in the history of aviation.

His twenty-second opponent was the famous Captain Ball,[28] by far the best English flier. Ball was as famous in his own time as was Major Hawker, whom I had already shot down some months ago. It made me especially happy that it was my brother who had dispatched England's second champion. Captain Ball flew a triplane and met my brother alone at the Front. Each tried to catch the other. Neither was fortunate enough to get behind his adversary. Then both separated and simultaneously decided to try a head-on attack. Each had the engine in front of him for protection. Both fired but the possibility of a hit was very slight, for the speed was twice as great as usual. It was really improbable that either one of them would score a hit, yet my brother, who was somewhat lower, stalled and flipped over. For some moments his machine was uncontrollable, but he soon recovered and found that his opponent had shot up both fuel tanks. He had to land. Quickly he turned the ignition off; otherwise, the crate would burn. But the next thought was, Where is my opponent? In the moment of turning over he had seen his opponent also rear up and turn over. Therefore, he could not be too far away. The dominating thought was, Is he above me or below me? Looking beneath him he saw the triplane plunging downward. It fell and fell, without starting again, until it smashed to pieces on the ground. It was on our territory. Both opponents had hit each other with their fixed

27 Famous prewar French stunt flier and wartime Ace

28 The British Royal Flying Corps records do not concur with the episode described here. Both the date of the encounter and the description of the aircraft differ. Ball was flying an S.E.5 on the day he disappeared.

machine guns in the brief moment of meeting. My brother had both his fuel tanks shot up, and at the same moment Captain Ball was shot in the head. He carried on him some photographs and newspaper clippings from his hometown, where he had been honored while on leave a short time before. In Boelcke's time Ball had destroyed thirty-six German machines. Now he had met his master. Was it by chance that a man as great as he must also die a normal man's death?

Captain Ball was quite certainly the leader of the Anti-Richthofen Squadron, and I believe the English would have preferred to give up trying to catch me. That would have made us unhappy for they provided us with many beautiful fighting opportunities when they were at it.

If my brother had not been wounded on the fifth of May, I believe that after my return from leave he would likewise have gone on leave with fifty-two to his credit.

LOTHAR A "SHOOTER" AND NOT A HUNTER

My father makes a distinction between a hunter, a sportsman, and a shooter whose only fun is shooting. Early in the war I found that when I downed an Englishman, my hunting passion was quenched for the time being. I seldom tried to shoot down two Englishmen, one right after another. If one fell, I had the feeling of absolute satisfaction. Only much, much later did I overcome that and also became a shooter.

It was different with my brother. I had an opportunity to observe him when he shot down his fourth and fifth opponents. We attacked a squadron. I was the first to single out an adversary, and my opponent was soon dispatched. I looked around and saw that my brother sat behind an English machine from which flames shot out. Near this Englishman flew a second. Lothar did nothing further to the first, who had not yet fallen and was still in the air. He turned his machine gun on the next one and immediately shot at him after he had barely finished with the other. This one also fell after a short battle.

At home he asked quite proudly: "How many have you shot down?" I said quite modestly: "One." He turned his back to me and said: "I got two." I sent him up forward to determine what the fellows' names were, etc. Late in the afternoon he came back after having found only one.

Consequently, the inquiry was difficult, as it usually is with such shooters. However, a day later the troops reported where the other lay and confirmed what we had all seen.

The Aurochs

In an opportune moment during a visit to Headquarters, the Prince of Pless invited me to hunt bison with him. The bison is the animal which is commonly called the aurochs. The true aurochs is extinct, but the bison resembles him to a great extent. There are only two places on the whole earth where they are found, in Pless and in the hunting preserve of the former Czar in the Bialowicz Forest. The Bialowicz Forest has, of course, suffered tremendously through the war. Many good bison that would otherwise have been shot only by princely personages and the Czar, have been brought down by a musketeer.

Through the kindness of His Highness, therefore, I was allowed to shoot so rare an animal. In about a generation there will be no more, for they will have been exterminated.

I arrived at Pless on the afternoon of the twenty-sixth of May and immediately set out from the station. I was impatient to kill a bull that same evening. We traveled along the famous road through the enormous wildlife preserve of the Prince, which many crowned heads before me had traveled. After about an hour's drive we got out and had to walk for half an hour in order to come to the shooting place. During this time the drivers were already placed waiting for the signal to begin the hunt. I stood on the high point where, the head forester reported to me, many noblemen had already stood to bag a great number of bison. We waited quite some time. Then suddenly I saw, in the high timber, a giant black monster trundling along right toward me. I saw this even before the forester. I got ready to shoot and, I must say, I had hunting fever. It was a mighty bull—two hundred fifty paces away. He sniffed the air for a moment. I was too far away to shoot. Perhaps I would have hit the monster, as one generally does not miss something so gigantic. But searching for it would have been an unpleasant task as well as a disgrace if I had missed him. Therefore, I preferred to wait until he came closer. He probably noticed the drivers, for suddenly he made a sharp turn and came directly toward me at a remarkable speed for such an animal. It was a bad angle for a shot. Then he disappeared behind a group of thick spruce. I heard him snorting and stamping, but I could no longer see him. I did not know if he had got wind of me or not. In any event, he was gone. I saw him once again from a great distance, then he disappeared.

Whether it was the unusual view of such an animal, or who knows what—in any case, I had in that moment, when the bull came at me, the same feeling, the same hunting fever that grips me when I sit in an airplane, see an Englishman, and must fly along for five minutes to come at him. The difference is that the Englishman defends himself. If I had not stood on so high a platform, who knows what feelings would have taken charge!

It did not take long for a second bull to come along. He was also a mighty fellow. He made it much easier for me. About a hundred paces away he sniffed the air and showed his whole shoulder to me. The first shot was a hit. A month before, Hindenburg had said to me: "Take many bullets with you. I used half a dozen on mine, for such a fellow does not die easily. The heart lies so deeply in him that most times one shoots past it." And that was so. I had not hit the heart, even though I know exactly where it lies. I shot again, and then a third time, until he finally stayed where he was, mortally wounded. He was perhaps fifty paces away from me. Five minutes later the monster was finished. The hunt ended and a successful kill was trumpeted. All three bullets were right over his heart—a sign of very good shooting.

We now drove past the beautiful hunting lodge of the Prince and through the wildlife preserve in which every year at hunting time the guests of the Prince killed their red deer, etc. We stopped and looked at the inside of the house in Promnitz. It is located on a peninsula with a marvelous view; there are no human beings for a distance of five kilometers. One no longer has the feeling of being in a wildlife preserve, as generally imagined, when speaking of a hunt with the Prince of Pless. Four hundred thousand acres of fenced-in area are no longer a hunting preserve. It is a wilderness. There are splendid deer, the like of which no one has ever seen but the foresters, that are killed as the opportunity arises during hunting season. One can walk for weeks without coming face to face with a bison. During many seasons it is impossible to even see them. For they are so stealthy they are completely hidden in the gigantic forests and unending thickets. We saw many antlered deer and many good rams.

About two hours later we reached Pless, shortly before dark.

Wounded

On a splendid day (6 July 1917) I took off on a pursuit flight with my *Jagdstaffel*. We roared around quite a while between Ypres and Armentières without getting into a fight.

Then I saw an enemy squadron in the distance and thought: Our "friends" are coming over to play. They came to the Front, saw us, but turned back again, and I thought we had scared them away. Therefore I decided to use cunning to tempt them back. I pretended to fly away, while constantly watching the enemy squadron. It did not take long before I saw them again flying in the direction of the Front.

We had an unfavorable east wind, so I let them fly a great distance inland before cutting off their retreat to the Front. It was again my dear friends, the great Vickers, which is an English airplane with a lattice-type fuselage; the observer sits up forward.[29]

We slowly followed our swift enemy toward the Front. We would probably never have gotten them if we had not had greater altitude from which to come down on them. After a while I had the rearmost machine close enough in front of me to consider all the possible ways to attack him. Wolff flew beneath me. I could see from the position of the handle of his machine gun that he was ready to get into battle. Then my opponent went into a nosedive and maneuvered to take up the fight with me. But, in spite of everything, it was from such a great distance that one could not call it true aerial combat. I had not yet flicked the safety off my gun, as there still was time until I could get close enough to do battle with my opponent. Then I watched as the observer, obviously excited, shot at me. I calmly let him fire, for his best marksmanship would not have helped at a distance of over three hundred meters. One just does not score at that distance! Now he turned on me completely and I hoped to get behind him in the next turn to burn his hide. Suddenly I received a blow to my head! I was hit! For a moment my whole body was completely paralyzed. My hands dropped to the side and my legs dangled

---

[29] The Germans called all enemy two-seat "pusher" aircraft (i.e., with the engine mounted behind the cockpit) "Vickers" machines, although they were indeed of many different types.

in the fuselage. The worst part was that the blow on the head affected my optic nerve and I was completely blinded. The machine plunged down. For a moment it flashed through my mind that this is the way it looks just before death. I doubted that the wings could stand the strain, and I expected they would break off at any moment.

I was alone in the crate. I did not lose consciousness immediately. I fought to regain control of my arms and legs so that I could grasp the control stick. I managed to shut off the gas and the ignition. But would that alone help me! I had moved my eyes around and taken my goggles off, but it was not even possible to see the sun. I was completely blinded. The seconds were an eternity to me. I noticed that I continued to fall. The machine had gone back and forth but always came back to a dive. At the beginning I was at an altitude of four thousand meters, and now I must have fallen at least two or three thousand meters. I gathered up all my energy and said to myself: "I must see!" I don't know if the effort helped, but in any case, I suddenly could distinguish black and white spots before me. My eyesight came back more and more. I peered at the sun and could look at it freely without experiencing even the slightest pain or feeling; it was as if I had been blindfolded. Now it was like looking through thick black glasses. But it was enough.

My first view was of the altimeter. It showed eight hundred meters. I had no idea where I was. I started the engine again, brought the airplane around to a normal altitude and set my glide path. Nothing but shell holes lay beneath me. To my great joy, I recognized a great forest complex and determined from this that I was already a bit on our side of the lines. Had the Englishman followed me he could have shot me down without blinking an eye. But, thank God, I found myself protected by my comrades, who from the start could not understand my falling and diving.

At this point I wanted to land, as I did not know how long

I could hold out before fainting. I went down to fifty meters, but I could not find even a tiny place among the many shell craters where it might be possible to make a landing. I gave the engine the gas and decided to fly east at low altitude for as long as I remained conscious. At the beginning it went quite well, but after some seconds I noticed that my power was weakening and gradually everything got black before me. Now was the time to land. I set the machine down quickly and smoothly, taking with it some poles and telephone wires that looked all the same to me in that moment. I lacked the strength to stand up in my machine. I tried to climb out, and in so doing, I fell. I just lay there.

Some people arrived immediately. They had observed the whole incident and knew from the red machine who I was. The enlisted men wrapped up my head with first-aid-kit bandages. What happened next is only a vague memory. I had not entirely lost consciousness, but I found myself in a drowsily confused condition. I only know that I had just lain on a thistle and no longer found the strength to roll off, which in the long run was most painful.

I was lucky enough to have landed my machine near a road. It did not take long before I was placed in an ambulance and transported to a field hospital in Courtrai after many hours of travel. The doctors had already got everything ready and now began their work.

I had quite a respectable hole in my head, a wound of about ten centimeters in length that was, of course, later drawn together; but in one place clear white bone as big as a *Taler*[30] remained exposed. My thick Richthofen head once again proved itself. The skull had not been penetrated. With some imagination one could ascertain a swelling in the X-ray photos. It was an unpleasant skull fracture that did not get better for days.

[30] A large, silver German coin, similar to the American silver dollar

It was reported at home that I lay in the hospital with severe head and chest wounds, but in other respects all went quite well for me.

I was curious about who would be able to get into the air again first, my brother or I. My brother was afraid it would be me, and I was afraid it would be my brother.

(A LETTER)

In the Field

Arrived here again, working industriously. I have just shot down number fifty-three. In Kreuznach, on the way back, I was invited by His Majesty to meet the King of Bulgaria, who presented me the Cross of Bravery, First Class. It is worn like the Iron Cross, First Class, and looks very good. I met the Chancellor, Count Dohna, and some other ministers.

Concerning Oscar, I have now positively determined that he is dead, for he fell or jumped out of his airplane in the last five hundred meters. He lies near the Front, but on the other side. Through notes dropped to the Englishmen, I have tried to determine if his body could be recovered. In this respect the Royal Flying Corps is very noble.

I attended Schäfer's funeral. I flew from Berlin to Krefeld in three hours; it takes eight hours by train.

Yesterday, unfortunately, Georg Zeumer fell in aerial combat. Perhaps it was best for him, for he knew that the end of his life was approaching. This splendid, pleasant fellow! It would have been terrible if he had to be slowly tormented until death. It was a hero's death. In the next few days his body will be brought home.

I visited Lothar (in the hospital) and arrived just before he was moved. He looked splendid, tanned and already dressed and lying on his couch, with the *Pour le mérite* around his neck. He can stand now and is quite restored to health. He will be able to walk and ride well again. He should be able to return to the field in about two months. But first he should have a good rest.

(A LETTER)

Jagdgeschwader, 28 August 1917

I am very happy about Lothar's health. Under no circumstances should he be allowed back at the Front until he is physically fit. Otherwise he will suffer a relapse or be shot down. I noticed that I'm not quite right myself. I have just made two patrols. Of course, both were successful, but after each one I was completely exhausted. During the first one something almost happened to me. My wound is healing frightfully slow; it is still about as big as a five-mark piece. Yesterday they removed yet another piece of bone; I believe it will be the last.

A few days ago the Kaiser was here to review the troops, in the course of which he had a long conversation with me. I am going on leave shortly, and I am looking forward to being together with all of you.

Infantry, Artillery and Reconnaissance Fliers

If I had not been a fighter pilot, I believe I would have selected flying as an infantry observer. It is a great satisfaction for one to give direct assistance to our hardest fighting troops. The observer-pilot is in a position to do this. He has a much appreciated task in this assignment. I saw many excellent pilots during the battle of Arras, flying in all kinds of weather, at all times of the day, at low altitude over the enemy in support of our hard-fighting infantry. I can understand how one could be so impassioned as to cheer loudly, as I believe so many observers did when they saw the enemy troops falling back before a hand-to-hand attack by our dashing infantry charging out of the trenches. After many a pursuit flight I fired my remaining bullets into the enemy trench emplacements. Even if it is of little help, it makes an impression on their morale.

I myself have been an artillery spotter. During my time it was somewhat novel to direct the firing of our own artillery by wireless telegraph. But it takes a special ability to do it. I could not adapt to it for long. I prefer combat. To do artillery flying one must belong to the artillery branch of service in order to do the most effective work.

I have also done reconnaissance flying, particularly in Russia during the trench fighting. Then I was a cavalryman again, that is, I came down a peg when I rode in my steel Pegasus. Each day of flight with Holck over the Russians is among my fondest memories. But the flavor of the old excitement does not come back.

In the West the reconnaissance flier sees things quite differently than the eye of the cavalry is accustomed to. The villages and cities, the trains and streets look so dead and still; and, although there is often heavy traffic on them, it is often concealed from the flier. Only a very practiced eye is capable of observing with accuracy from high altitudes. I have good eyes, but I doubt that anyone can recognize much detail on a road from an altitude of five thousand meters. Therefore, the observer's eye is replaced by photographic apparatus; one photographs what one thinks is important and what one is ordered to photograph. If one comes home and the photographic plates are spoiled, the whole flight has been in vain.

It often happens that the observation flier becomes involved in a fight, but he has more important things to do than busy himself with combat. Often a photographic plate is more important than shooting down an enemy machine, and for that reason he is not blamed in most cases for not fighting in the air.

It is a different task nowadays to accomplish a good reconnaissance mission in the West.

Our Airplanes

It is indeed quite evident that in the course of the war our airplanes have changed somewhat. The greatest difference is the extremes in size between the giant airplanes and the fighter planes.

The fighter plane is small, fast and maneuverable, but carries only bullets and machine guns.

The giant airplane—one simply must view the captured English giant airplane[31] that landed without damage on our side—is a colossus, destined to carry as much weight as possible on its great wings. It will haul a tremendous amount of bombs and fuel, and distances of three thousand to five thousand kilograms are nothing at all for it. The fuel tanks are just like railway tank cars. One no longer has the feeling of flying in so great a machine; rather, one "travels." Flying is no longer done through feeling, but through technical instruments instead.

Such a giant airplane has tremendous horsepower. I do not know the precise number, but it is many thousand. The more, the better. It is not out of the question that we could even transport a whole division in such a thing. One can go for a walk inside the fuselage. In one of its sections the technicians have incredibly built in a wireless telegraph with which someone in flight can be in contact with someone on the ground. In another section hang the beautiful "smoked sausages," the

[31] A Handley Page 0/400 bomber

famous bombs which those below fear so much. Gun barrels jut from every section. It is a flying fortress. The wings with their struts look like a portico. But I cannot get inspired by these giant barges. I find them monstrous, unsportsmanlike, boring and clumsy. I prefer an airplane such as *"Le petit rouge"*; with such a plane one can fly over on one's back, or fly upside-down, or do whatever other tricks one can perform. One flies just like a bird, but it is not "winged flight" like the albatross; rather, the whole thing is just a flying engine. I believe we will come so far that for two and a half marks we will be able to buy a flying suit into which one will simply crawl. In one end will be a little engine and little propeller, the arms will go in the wings, the legs in the tail, then one will hop a bit to start and go into the air like a bird.

You are certainly laughing, dear reader, and so am I, but it may come to pass that our children will not laugh. People also laughed fifty years ago when they were told someone would fly over Berlin. I remember the excitement in the year 1910 when Count Zeppelin first came to Berlin, and now the Berliners scarcely look up when something sails through the air. Besides the giant airplanes and the planes for fighter pilots, there are countless numbers of others in every size. Man has yet to come to the end of discovery. Who knows what we will use in a year's time to pierce the blue ether!

It Is Only in the Fight

The commander of a *Jagdgeschwader* must stay with his unit. It is not feasible for him to live somewhere in the rear area and communicate by telephone to his fliers the orders theoretically laid out on the green table in the support area. That will not do! The commander of the *Jagdgeschwader*[32]

---

[32] Fighter group comprised of four *Jagdstaffeln*, or fighter squadrons

must be in close contact with each of his squadron leaders, who are his subordinates, and must even know each single fighter pilot of a squadron through personal observation of his abilities. Flying before the enemy is not as easy as arranging things on a table; a qualified fighter pilot is one who attacks the enemy when he sees him, who is ready and capable of engaging in combat at all times and does not give thought as to whether he may be lying on the ground with his shattered machine at the end of the battle. Many gentlemen wearing beautiful uniforms have gone down to their death; it takes more than a uniform to make a fighter pilot. There are no longer any well-dressed fighter pilots.

The commander of a *Jagdgeschwader* must understand how to separate the chaff from the wheat. He can only do that when he is constantly with the men he commands.

But not only that. The commander of a *Jagdgeschwader* must himself be a fighter pilot and, indeed, not only a good one but a successful one. He must fly with them. Why? Because he must observe how his gentlemen fight. That is most important of all. He must know which men to place together in a squadron flight. He must be able to judge which ones will fight well together in the air. The other fighter squadrons at the Front that get anywhere consist of comrades who are well coordinated with one another and who all know well that no one will leave the other in the lurch when the situation becomes precarious.

Comradeship is actually the big thing in a *Jagdstaffel*. I will not put up with a stinker, unless he can also be a useful man against the enemy.

The commander of a *Geschwader* should not boss his fighter squadrons around too much. The squadron leader must have unconditional freedom in the territory allotted to him. During important moments the commander of fighter squadrons should direct their main areas of battle without, as it seems, having to prescribe that one must "fly through three times" in a certain time period. Such orders are outright nonsense. The fighter pilots should have an allotted area to cruise around in as it suits them, but when they see an opponent they must attack and shoot him down. Anything else is absurd. Nothing else matters to us but the aerial victory. Good old Herr Clausewitz has already said that in war nothing else makes sense but the destruction of the opposition. If someone claims that it is the role of the fighter pilots to patrol a certain area at the Front to deter the opposition from undertaking observation and reconnaissance flights, he is wrong. The mastery of the air in war is won through nothing other than battle, that is, shooting down the enemy. Besides, that kind of order has a devastating effect on some fighter pilots whose nerves may not be too strong and whose will to fight is easily weakened. One of the somewhat careful fighter pilots has already said: "You accomplish the same thing when you fly back and forth at the Front as when you attack and destroy the enemy." This somewhat questionable "fighter" pilot will be completely useless when the battle is joined. Our superior commanders should realize that the outcome of the war does not depend on well-written orders. It is only in the fight that the battle is won.

Der Rote Kampfflieger

Each day since the publication of my book, I have received many letters and cards from people who write how much they like *Der Rote Kampfflieger*.[33] That really makes me very happy. I read them all, but I doubt if I can reply to half of

---

[33] These observations were written for publication in a second edition, which was published in 1933.

them. I have given great effort to writing as many people as possible.

It is very amusing to see the various impressions the book makes on different readers. For instance, a comrade who is probably a great glutton and who is obviously profiting from the war writes:

"Very honored comrade, please write to me immediately where you managed to obtain oysters. I would also like to eat oysters."

I laughed so hard when I received this letter, I had to hold my sides. I vaguely remembered mentioning oysters, but this honored comrade had taken the oyster affair for the quintessence of the book.

A schoolboy sent me a hand mirror and noted that he had concluded from the book that I was lacking such an instrument in my red airplane.

I received an extraordinary amount of mail from the Cadet Corps. The cadets write me that they share my opinions of teachers. Theirs also give them trouble, and they learn only what is most necessary in order to be promoted.

My youngest brother, Bolko, wrote a long letter of complaint to the family. He is a cadet in Wahlstatt and complains that I portrayed the teachers in the Cadet Corps badly in my book. He is having so much unpleasantness in the Corps that he can no longer bear it. He asks the family to see to it that I first submit the manuscript of my next book for his approval. I think he demands quite a bit of me, good Bolko, besides accusing me of lies. I related that I once clambered up the church tower in Wahlstatt and hung a handkerchief there. Bolko has established beyond a doubt that the handkerchief no longer hangs there, and that because of that I could scarcely have told the truth. I think it is asking too much of a handkerchief to adorn a church tower for fifteen years.

Someone sent me the London *Times*. The newspaper carried a discussion of *Der Rote Kampfflieger*. I think it is quite ticklish to review something from the other side during the war, although I come off quite well in the discussion. Consequently, if I should fall into English captivity, the Lords will surely treat me decently.

But many times such a book also acts catastrophically on the emotions of some people. An unfortunate person wrote me that she idolizes me. She has already read my book seven times. Poor child!

Something else happened that is quite amazing. I received a letter from a young lady who wrote that she came from a well-known family. This lady is a novice and will become a nun. She hung a picture of me that she had picked up somewhere, in her cell in the convent. One day the abbess came into the cell and saw the picture. The novice received a severe reprimand and was told that prospective nuns should not have pictures of men hanging in their cells—even when these men are fighter pilots. The novice, therefore, had to remove the picture. But what did the clever child do? She did something that perhaps flatters, if not misrepresents, me. She wrote to a friend who was also a nun and asked her to send a large photograph of herself. When the friend did that, the young lady cut the face out of the photograph and stuck my face under the nun's habit.

I heard the following splendid story:

Two English publishers want to bring out *Der Rote Kampfflieger* in England. Both have gone to the London Patent Office because it deals with the publication of books in England that are in violation of international copyright agreements. The representative of the authorized English body did me a great honor. He explained that the book has both great general and professional interest and that its publication in English would be useful, for it describes the method in which the best German fighter pilot had shot down Captain

Ball, the most famous English flier. Therefore, *Der Rote Kampfflieger* will appear in England when both publishers have come to terms.

God save the King!

Thoughts in a Dugout

Hanging from the ceiling in my dugout is a lamp I had made, as a conversation piece, from the engine of an airplane I shot down. I mounted small lamps in the cylinders, and when I lie awake at nights and let the light burn, Lord knows this chandelier looks fantastic and weird. When I lie that way, I have much to think about. I write this without knowing if anyone outside of my closest relatives will ever see it. I am occupied with thoughts of continuing *Der Rote Kampfflieger* and, indeed, for quite a good reason. The battle now taking place on all Fronts has become awfully serious; there is nothing left of the "lively, merry war," as our deeds were called in the beginning. Now we must fight off despair and arm ourselves so that the enemy will not penetrate our country. I now have the gravest feeling that people have been exposed to quite another Richthofen than I really am. When I read my book, I smile at the insolence of it. I now no longer possess such an insolent spirit. It is not because I'm afraid, though one day death may be hard on my heels; no, it's not for that reason, although I think enough about it. One of my superiors advised me to give up flying, saying it will catch up with me one day. But I would become miserable if now, honored with glory and decorations, I became a pensioner of my own dignity in order to preserve my precious life for the nation while every poor fellow in the trenches endures his duty exactly as I did mine.

I am in wretched spirits after every aerial battle. But that no doubt is an aftereffect of my head wound. When I set foot on the ground again at my airfield after a flight, I go to my quarters and do not want to see anyone or hear anything. I think of this war as it really is, not as the people at home imagine, with a Hoorah! and a roar. It is very serious, very grim . . .

MEMORIES OF MY BROTHER

BY

Lothar Freiherr von Richthofen

The Red Color

It became known all over that the English had put a price on my brother's head. Every flier over there knew him, for at the time he alone flew a red airplane. For that reason we wanted to paint every airplane in our squadron, and we pleaded with my brother not to be so conspicuous. The request was granted, for through our many victories we had shown ourselves worthy of the color. The color red signified a certain arrogance. Everyone knew that. It attracted attention. Hence, one had to accomplish something. We looked with pride on our red birds. My brother's crate was glaring red. The rest of us each had his own special mark painted in other colors. In the air one cannot see another flier's face, so we chose these colors as recognition insignia. For example, Schäfer had the elevator, rudder and rear part of the fuselage in black, Allmenröder had the same in white, Wolff had green, and I had yellow. As a yellow dragooneer, that was the appointed color for me. Each had a different mark. In the air the entire machine appeared red to those on the ground as well as to the enemy fliers, for only a small part of the machine was painted a second color. Those who took part in the defensive battle of Arras saw much of the red birds and their work.

Why did *Rittmeister* Von Richthofen paint his crate red? The French labeled this as a childish affectation in one newspaper article. The real reason lies elsewhere. When Manfred began to gain his first successes with *Jagdstaffel Boelcke,* he was annoyed because he felt he was much too visible to his enemies in aerial combat and that they saw him much too early. He tried using a variety of colors to make himself invisible. At first he emphasized the earth colors. From above one would not detect these colors if there were no movement, which is of course impossible in a plane. To his sorrow, Manfred found that no one color was useful in the air. There is no camouflage for the flier with which he can make himself invisible. Then, in order to at least be recognized as the leader by his comrades in the air, he chose the color bright red. Later the red machine also became known to the English as *"Le petit rouge"* and the other names that accompanied it. At one time it was maintained that a "Joan of Arc," or a woman of similar stature, sat in it. But soon both friend and enemy knew who sat in the red machine. An unaccountable enthusiasm was kindled in our troops at the Front, that was not shared by the enemy. It was similar to waving a red cloth before a bull to rashly provoke him. But with *"Le petit rouge"* that parallel ceases, for as soon as the English saw the red machine they made themselves scarce. Thus, in the battle of Arras the red machine had only to approach the Front in order to send the English fleeing to their own lines.

Cut Off

In time one flies over many Fronts. The incident that I now relate took place near Cambrai, when during marvelous weather I flew with my brother to the Front.

In the north puffs of smoke were to be seen. As we two

came near the lines, a single English plane flew back over the Front to his own lines. For the time being there was nothing else to be seen. We flew over the English lines without being fired at. There was an east wind which was very favorable for an aerial battle. In battle one drifts with the strong wind. The single-seater has the advantage only in the attack. That is a result of his armament [machine guns that fire forward]. In an aerial battle, if one is carried far over enemy territory by the wind, the moment must come when it becomes necessary to fly back to one's lines, and to do this one must go on the defensive. For the single-seater fighter that can fire only forward, it is a very fateful moment, which for many becomes disastrous!

Suddenly my brother and I saw five Englishmen who were coming down on us from a great height. In flying with others I have never had the same feeling of superiority as when I flew with my brother. And this time was no different.

At the moment they did not venture to come too close to us, but, rather, they remained above us and took practice shots. Then one became somewhat bolder and pounced on me. A quick turn and I sat behind him. The hunter became the prey. The Englishman tried to save himself by flying west. Through continuous zigzag flying he did not offer me a sure target. Then he ceased his defensive movements. The observer appeared to me to be wounded. The Englishman already "stunk," a flying expression for the ribbon of smoke from a punctured fuel or oil tank. I was just ready to give the Englishman a final burst when my guns jammed. Deeply sorry, I let him go and turned away. In the course of the battle I had strayed many kilometers from our Front. Suddenly a frightful thought came to me: Where are the other four Englishmen and where is my brother? Then I saw a ghastly scene! The four Englishmen and my brother were turning circles around each other in a wild battle. I was fearful for Manfred. I had a gun jam and could no longer shoot. But he must have help! After all, my brother had continuously distracted the four Englishmen, who would have long since cut me off. Now it was my turn to help. I got right in the middle of the combatants. The four Englishmen, who had previously had one opponent, suddenly left us and flew home, even though they were double our number. They could not have known that my guns were jammed as well. As my brother said afterwards, he had given up on both our lives.

Schäfer Saves My Life

In peacetime one would have received the Lifesaving Medal for it, but in wartime I was only able to give Schäfer a bottle of champagne at supper for what he had done for me. It was splendid weather with blue skies, and we took off on the basis of a report that there was enemy aerial activity at the Front. There were Schäfer and I and two other gentlemen. At first we saw nothing at the Front. Nevertheless, we knew there must be Englishmen about. We did see five great, deep-fuselage biplanes, all two-seaters, but unfortunately, very far away. We flew over the Front, up toward the five Englishmen far on the other side. The affair already began to get boring because the Englishmen would not come into our vicinity of the Front. We flew at about three thousand meters, then I discovered a single Englishman flying about a thousand meters below us. Better than nothing! Just as I began to go down in a dive, the Englishman, unfortunately, discovered the danger and fled. I took after him, although I was already many kilometers on his side of the lines. We were now down to fifteen hundred meters, but the Englishman withdrew from danger by going even lower. We were by this time five kilometers on the other side of the lines. Consequently, the battle was too unfavorable for me. I broke off, for a single shot in the engine would have been enough to force me to land on the other side.

Deeply depressed, I flew back in the direction of the Front. Suddenly one of the five Englishmen we had observed previously separated from the others and came after me. I was now very far on the other side, about five kilometers at a thousand-meter altitude, which for a single-seater that can fire only forward is the most unfavorable position imaginable. Consequently, I continued on toward the Front. When he was about a thousand meters away from me, the Englishman began to fire. This was unfavorable for him, for from that distance he could hit nothing! I calmly flew on. I continually heard the clatter of machine guns a great distance behind me. In the greatest hope I said to myself: Just wait, when they get close all their bullets will be used up and their guns will jam. Then suddenly I felt a hit in my machine! A main control wire was shot through. As a result, I could no longer make sharp turns for fear the wings would not stay together. Now, even without the Englishman on my neck, I would really have to crash. I was still three kilometers on the other side of the lines. No one knows the despair a flier feels at such times. In most cases one is not fully conscious of the danger when flying. My philosophy has always been: Take the war calmly.

Meanwhile, the Englishman was approaching at closer range. The machine-gun clatter was awfully loud, the phosphorous ammunition—incendiary bullets—flew all around me. I sat right in the stream of fire. It was horrible! I could not shoot, because the Englishman was right above me. Except for the danger that both wings would fly off, I would have made a sharp turn in order to get behind the Englishman myself. I felt quite clearly that my machine could no longer stand the strain, for it was almost a total wreck. In my thoughts I saw it burning in the next few seconds. Almost motionless, I hung like a practice target below the Englishman. But what did I see there? The English airplane was ablaze, and behind him flew a German airplane! Thank God!

I would have bet that within the next half minute I would have been shot down or that the wings would have fallen off. Arriving back home I merely gave Schäfer my hand and invited him that night to have a bottle of champagne. It was good that one could at least do that.

For my tenth victory, I had received an autographed picture of my brother. This was just three days before the morning Schäfer came to my rescue. In the afternoon I shot down number eleven near Vimy as proof that my mishap of the same day was caused by only a defect in my machine.

A Trick

One splendid, warm April morning we stood in front of our birds and waited for the alert. Then the telephone rattled. Brisk aerial activity south of Arras! A signal from the crew chief, the alarm bell sounds, and suddenly things come to life! The mechanics hurry from all corners to warm up the machines, which are placed near each other. The pilots also hurry along. Which is the lead airplane? My brother! Take off! Arriving south of Arras at about a three-thousand-meter altitude—nothing is to be seen! Suddenly there are three Englishmen. To our amazement, the three attack us by pouncing on us from a higher altitude. My brother takes on the first, Wolff the second, and I the third. As long as the Englishman is above me, he shoots. I must wait until he comes down to my altitude in order to shoot at him. And so, now he is near me. I will shoot right away, and he will try to fool me and go into a spin. And I think: I can do that also. I slip sideways ten meters and likewise go into a spin. Now he flies straight ahead again. Then I am sitting behind him. As soon as he spots me, he begins to make wild turns. We have the west wind in our favor; therefore, the battle that began at the Front must take place ever more on our side of the line. Consequently, I follow him. As soon as he tries to fly straight, I give him some warning shots. Finally the situation becomes boring. I try to hit him in the turns, and shoot and shoot.

We were by now deep behind our lines at an altitude of about five hundred meters. I forced the Englishman to make more turns. While turning in an air fight one drops lower and lower until he must land, or attempt to fly straight home. My Englishman decided to do the latter. Lightning-quick the thought came to me: Now the hour for this poor fellow has come! I sat behind him. At the necessary distance, about fifty meters away, I sighted him cleanly and pressed my machine-gun buttons. What next! Not a shot came out. A jam in the guns. I cleared them and again pressed the machine-gun buttons: Not a shot! Curses! Success so near! I looked at my machine guns once more. Blast! I had already shot my last round. I have the empty ammunition belts in my hands. A thousand shots! I had so many when I did not need them.

Under no circumstances could I allow him to get away, however. To have fought with a red machine for almost a quarter of an hour and to have escaped—that would be a triumph for the English!

I flew closer and closer to him, the distance from my propeller to his rudder constantly decreasing. I estimated: ten meters, five meters, three, now only two meters! Finally a perplexing thought came to me: Shall I strike his rudder with my propeller? Then he would fall, but I would probably go with him. Another thought: If I shut the engine off the minute I touch him, what would happen? Then my Englishman looked around at me, saw me directly behind him, cast a terrified glance at me, shut his engine off, and landed near our third position. Down on the ground he let his engine idle.

When one lands near the enemy, a pilot tries to set fire to his airplane to destroy it. In order to prevent this, one shoots in the vicinity of the airplane in such cases until the pilot runs away. So I flew over so close to his head that he noticed I was on the alert. The Englishman jumped out of his machine, waved to me and held his hands high, and let himself be taken by our infantry nearby.

In his defense, I must say the Englishman could not have known that I had no more bullets. One shot would have been enough at such close range to hit him. But he needed only to turn around and I would have had to run away. At most he fired only fifty shots at me, while I was completely defenseless without bullets. But the affair was successful, that is the main point. The next day I flew to the sector where the airplane, a Spad, a very good English[1] single-seater at the time, had been taken for safety; I looked at the machine and searched for hits. With my thousand shots I must have hit him at least once! I asked if the passenger was wounded, whereupon the answer promptly came: "No!" Not a single hit was to be found on the whole of the plane. Not even the axle was bent, which, moreover, could easily have happened in a bad landing or on unfavorable terrain! Now I had to laugh. The Englishman had landed actually out of fear of me!

In my victory list today it says: "On 29 April 1917 in the morning near Izel, a Spad single-seater, passenger an English officer." I did not speak with him, as our airfield was far away from his landing place, so he never learned that I had had no more bullets and that he landed merely out of fear. Arriving at home with my squadron, I doubted that I could bring myself to tell anyone that with a thousand shots I had not scored a single hit!

My brother and Wolff had shot down both of theirs. I am not sure that I did not really tell anyone in the squadron, I was so ashamed at the time of my poor marksmanship. With this opportunity it is interesting to mention how many shots

[1] The Spad was of French design and manufacture, although some were built in England.

one generally needs to shoot down an Englishman. When I
flew with my brother the first time and watched, I noticed
that hardly had my brother begun to fire when the Englishman fell. In general, my brother did not use more than twenty
shots. But one cannot do that as a rule. One mainly attacks
an Englishman from behind in order to shoot in the direction
of flight. If the Englishman flies straight ahead and a good
marksman sits behind him, then the Englishman will fall during the first shots. But if the opponent begins to twist and
turn, then the chances of hitting him are slim.

Crashed

The thirteenth of March! At the Front there was no difference between Sunday and a weekday. Many times one did not
know one day from another, so I had not thought at all that
the thirteenth would really be my unlucky day. Our squadron
flew to the Front that day under the leadership of my brother.
More reports of brisk aerial activity had been prepared for
us. We had scarcely arrived at the Front when we met a
swarm of Englishmen. Everyone chose an opponent and attacked him, so I did, too. I attacked my opponent in a dive.
Then I heard a loud crash within my machine! It was hit.
Only too late I noticed what was wrong. My Fokker triplane
suddenly became a biplane. It is a horrible feeling to be minus
one wing at four thousand meters. I quickly broke away from
my Englishman. He was really quite stupid and did not follow
me. Nothing would have been easier than to shoot me down
in this condition. With both remaining wings I could still
bring it into a normal glide, but only straight ahead, as the
rudder no longer functioned. Only in a glide could I keep the
machine at the necessary altitude. Before me lay a great open

space. I wanted to land there. While generally I could estimate in meters where I wanted to land the machine, this time
I made a mistake. When I was at five hundred meters I suddenly saw before me a high-tension wire. I could no longer
go over it and I could not go under it, because two columns of
men were moving along both sides of it. Therefore I had to
make a turn. But I was too low and it could no longer be
done!

Damn it all! I am lying in bed. Four sterile white walls! I
am in a field hospital with nurses around the bed. My head
is bound up and I cannot touch it. Aha! Now it dawns on
me: I wanted to land and make a turn! In the attempt to turn,
I crashed and lost consciousness. I had been hit only on the
head and legs. My hands were still on the control stick. As
my comrades said later, they had taken my crash for a death
plunge.

Bombing as an Observer

Before the single-seat fighter plane was known, it was
thought that the two-seater was the ultimate battle machine.
The so-called *Kampfgeschwader* [battle group] existed at the
time. When I went into aviation, I thought aerial combat was
the most exciting thing and I was happy when I was assigned
[as an observer] to a *Kampfgeschwader*. I trained daily in
aerial combat with my good pilot. Despite the numerous air
fights we participated in, we had no success. As this activity
was not satisfying enough, we set about dropping bombs. To
begin with, we practiced by dropping bombs on targets at
our airfield in my *Kampfgeschwader*.

While doing this a funny thing happened. One of the
officer observers was a nearsighted professor. We had laid out
a white cloth as a target. Each one flew over it and dropped

his eggs. Then the professor came down the line, his plane wavering to the target. Suddenly he saw something white beneath him and released his bombs. The bombs dropped and hit in the middle of a herd of cows in whose midst was a white cow. He bagged seven cows on this "raid," and he became the pride of our squadron! We had beef to eat for a week. From then on, the good professor was called "Cow Killer."

Cow Killer accomplished many other things. After his first operational flight he came home breathless, maintaining that air fighting was a very strenuous matter. A robust, broadshouldered man, he was completely tired out and red as a lobster, although aerial combat otherwise required no special physical effort. We could not account for this mystery until the following story came out: An observer has as armament one machine gun fixed to a ring. Cow Killer had taken his along unfastened and had fought with it freehand. This, of course, would account for his condition; it is indeed an enormous strain to use the machine gun freehand, especially when one considers the extraordinary flow of air in an airplane.

After sufficient practice, we dropped our bombs on the enemy. For that, one climbs to an altitude of three to four thousand meters on this side of the lines, crosses the Front and steers to the selected target. One flew in great squadrons so that he would not be molested by enemy airplanes. For the most part, we flew gaily over the flak, for the enemy wasted a lot of ammunition on us, which, at best, was shot too short or too high. It was hard to observe the results of the bombing at this altitude. One merely saw a tiny little puff of smoke where the bomb exploded. It was much more satisfying to bomb at night. We inquired which target was of importance and then made that our night's work. This activity was very interesting. At ten o'clock in the evening we loaded as many bombs as there was room for in the airplane and flew in the direction of the enemy troops and ammunition depots. At night the enemy cannot see you, and so we could come down to fifty to a hundred meters over the target and at this altitude observe the results splendidly. It was bright as day from the explosion of the bombs that illuminated the surroundings. One could easily discern barracks filled with enemy troops, and ammunition depots. Once we succeeded in blowing an ammunition depot into the air. A single bomb set it off. The explosion spread over the whole camp, which was about a quarter of a kilometer in diameter. It looked as though the column of smoke would reach an altitude of three thousand to four thousand meters. One depot set off another. The shaking of the ground was noticeable for a radius of a kilometer. The camp burned through the next day.

This work as bomber crewman was very satisfying. We were scarcely back from our first flight when our crate was again loaded with bombs and filled with fuel. Meanwhile, we sat in the officers' mess and drank to work up new courage. This went on three or four times a night. The last flight might start as late as five o'clock in the morning. The darkness remained until eight o'clock.

During one of these morning flights we were on the way back to the field when a thick ground fog hid every orientation point on the ground. We could judge where friend and enemy lay only from the flash of the guns. As the Front did not run in a straight line, we were not quite sure where we were about to land. We first made a fuss over the place where we wanted to land at about an altitude of ten meters. With great strain to the eye we tried to make out trees, trenches, and other obstacles. Then we prepared for the landing itself. A forced landing amid haziness is one of the most dangerous things one can do. In ground fog such landings usually end in a fatal crash. We were lucky. We barely missed a tree and came to rest a meter in front of a deep trench. We quickly turned the machine around to be in a good position for take-off, for we were not quite sure whether or not we landed near Joffre.[2] My pilot, *Leutnant* Kreutzmann, called to me that we really should not make the trip back without taking a prisoner with us. To my great regret, we found that we had landed on our side. Consequently, there were no prisoners to be had. We had imagined how great it would have been to bring back a Frenchman. But I was pleased, nevertheless, when we discovered that we had landed quite close to the airfield of my brother, who had then achieved his first success with *Jagdstaffel Boelcke.*

A Day with Jagdstaffel 11

The *Staffel* was divided into two flights, that is, half of the *Staffel* always flew together. One time my brother flew as squadron leader with one flight, the next time with the other. Schäfer led my flight and, besides me, there was Wolff, Allmenröder, and Lübbert. At the time, that was the preferred number for flying together. Later the whole group earned the *Pour le mérite,* with the exception of *Leutnant* Lübbert, who unfortunately had fallen before that time. He had already accomplished great things in our section. Only his death prevented our dear comrade from receiving the *Pour le mérite.* On the day of which I write the flight had gotten an early start—that is, from daybreak on we had to be ready to take off at any moment. We sat in the ready room between four and five o'clock all set to jump up, when the telephone rang: "Six Bristols from Arras to Douai." We dashed out to our planes and took off.

At three thousand meters there was a break in the clouds. We saw the Englishmen right under the cloud cover in the

[2] No doubt a reference to Field Marshal Joseph Joffre, celebrated French military strategist. In this case meaning the French in general.

vicinity of our airfield. My brother's red bird stood on the field ready to go, his mechanics nearby. There was nothing to be seen of my brother. We started off to catch the Englishmen, but the fellows flew so skillfully in the cloud cover that none of us could shoot one of them down. Whenever one was in range he disappeared either above or below into the clouds. This was my first air fight, and I was very proud as I began to make one of them "stink" in the fire of my machine gun. I had shot through his fuel tank; but in the next moment he disappeared into the clouds. Since almost all machines have a reserve tank, he probably switched on the other fuel tank. At any rate the fellow flew away. I was, of course, very disappointed that he did not fall, but, as my brother said afterward, that would be too much to expect from the first air fight.

We did not shoot any of them down, and we landed at our field after about an hour. My brother's red bird still stood on the field, but even from far away the work of the mechanics and the position of the machine showed that he had been in action. Back in the ready room, we were told: Yes, the *Rittmeister* had started about five minutes after the squadron. He had been in bed when the reports came. He had quickly put his flight suit on over his pajamas and was off. He returned after twenty minutes, and in that time had shot down an Englishman on this side of the lines. When we came back again, he was in bed, sleeping again, as if nothing had happened. Only some hits in his machine and reports which poured in about the airplane shot down gave evidence of his flight. We were all a bit ashamed; there were five of us, we had started earlier, landed later, and had brought down nothing. As we gathered for the second start near eight o'clock, my brother appeared. He joked about the Englishmen, these nightly disturbers of the peace who drummed peace-loving people out of their beds in the middle of the night. We heartily congratulated him and told him of our experiences while he told us of his. He had started directly for the Front, an Englishman dropped through the clouds right in front of him. In a few seconds the battle was decided. The Englishman plunged down burning on our side. We renewed our strength and courage by having breakfast and then put on our flying suits again.

The *Jagdfliegerei* [literally: hunting aviation, or pursuit flying] is rightly named, for it is certainly a hunt for enemy fliers. This type of quarry indeed has its permanent haunt, but he uses it at indeterminate times whenever possible. On this second flight of the day we were to be lucky. The English fighter pilots had just sat down to breakfast.

I made up my mind to always fly fifty meters distant from my brother, for I said to myself that in this way I would get the first shots. I always kept close behind him and was happy that it went so well. A lone English artillery-observation plane had flown over the Front. I had enough to do just flying my machine, and the others, as on the first time, had seen nothing of the Englishman. But my brother had seen him, nonetheless. Quite suddenly he put his machine into a dive. In a short time he was behind the Englishman, and at almost the same moment the English airplane fell apart. He had broken the wings with a burst of machine-gun fire. The rest of the Englishman looked as if someone had shaken out a sack of large and small bits of paper. I saw the picture from a distance of about a thousand meters, although I had wanted to remain close behind my brother. I was unsuccessful in doing this. We flew the same machines, that is, the same type of airplanes, with the same engines; therefore, the fault must lie with me.

Fast flying must first be learned correctly. Of course, one can fly slow and fast. One can fly so slow that he is almost standing still; to do this one must run the engine very slow and leave the controls in a neutral position; then the machine scarcely moves forward and stalls, that is, it gradually sinks, though continuing a forward movement. It is very unpleasant when the rudder does not react properly, as when there is little or no air pressure on it. Such a practice slow flight at low altitudes is not recommended for beginners. This is indeed the slowest flying.

Then one can always fly somewhat faster than normal speed. At normal speed the machine always rises. Now when I put the nose down, with the engine full out, I can reach considerable speed. Naturally, that is a very great strain on the machine and the engine. Too much speed can be dangerous. This must be the first lesson learned. It sounds very easy, but I know many who never learned it. But I hold this ability to fly at fast yet controlled speeds to be much more important than many another flying trick—for example, looping, which is somewhat more for spectators. It looks very nice, but has no value in combat. The purpose of looping is to astound the layman and is used mostly over the hometown or before spectators.

After the single Englishman who was at the Front was shot down, we flew home. After the flight we of course talked about the recently experienced air battles. It is a very comical picture in which everyone who describes an aerial combat flails his arms; we speak with our hands so that we can teach ourselves and say what we have done wrong or done right. These discussions usually followed the air fights. This way also my brother achieved his objective of welding together a more effective fighting unit. For example, when he took over the squadron only Wolff and Allmenröder were there. At the time both had no experience at all, and beginners in an air fight have more fear than love of fatherland. During those first days my brother flew with both men, attacked many Englishmen, and received an enormous amount of hits on his machine without having any success, as both of them did not help him. Of course, my brother came home somewhat angry about this, but he did not rebuke them; rather, he said not a word about it. As Wolff and Allmenröder, who both later earned the *Pour le mérite,* said to me: That did more than the most severe reprimand. After the discussion my brother resumed his squadron leader's duties. At noon we had a war correspondent with us. I don't know whether Manfred was admired more by his comrades or by the guest. Just after the meal it was usual, if aerial activity allowed, to take a half-hour afternoon rest; for, in the battle action then going on, many days we flew four to seven times. In order to carry on this way, the primary conditions were: eating, sleeping, and not a drop of alcohol.

Toward evening my brother shot down another English two-seater with the lattice fuselage. The airplane made a normal glide, although the crewmen had been mortally hit by many bullets. The airplane continued its glide onto the roof of a house and was smashed completely. Since it was right in the area, my brother drove us in a car to the crash site to learn the serial number of the airplane and other things. One half of the airplane hung from the roof, the other lay in the street. The Englishman had dropped bombs in the area, so the air fight was observed by many, and a crowd of men in field gray inspected the wreckage of the Englishmen. When we had learned everything we needed, we set out for home. Meanwhile my brother had been recognized by the soldiers, and we left the place amid thundering cheers!

Last Flight with Manfred

In the spring of 1918 there was keen aerial activity on the part of the Englishmen. It was a bad time for gaining victories. The English artillery and infantry fliers had to go ever deeper into our territory and flew many kilometers on our side, but these reconnaissance squadrons seldom came near us, and then only at tremendous altitudes, never under three thousand meters. I had just come back to the field, after having had an inflammation of the middle ear, and I wanted to shoot down Englishmen. As always, my brother was in good form.

We were waiting for reports one beautiful morning at the field, already to suit up for flying. But there were no reports at all of any major enemy activity. Only now and then a single Englishman was reported far on the other side. After having waited about restlessly for some time, we flew off in hopes of meeting Englishmen at the Front. This time we were on the right trail. Arriving at the Front we saw about ten Englishmen heading for our lines at a great altitude. Evidently they wanted to fly over the Front in order to do their reconnaissance work. As soon as we reached their altitude, five thousand five hundred meters, we proceeded to attack. As always, my brother was on them first; he attacked one and forced him to go down. The Englishman tried to get rid of his opponent by diving and turning. My brother was always behind him. He then forced him with more hits to land the crate near our field.

I had merely been an observer at the beginning of this fight and had seen that my brother had only the one opponent. In such cases one does not need help. Therefore I looked around for a victim of my own. To that end there was one especially suited for me about a hundred meters below, beneath the English squadron. I attacked him. However, it was not easy for me. I flew ahead of my squadron, which was only half as strong as the Englishmen, and intended to get right behind my opponent in order to finish him off, when I suddenly saw that I was surrounded by airplanes with English cockades. The Englishmen did not intend to leave their comrade in the lurch and attacked me. I made a long dive of about a hundred meters in order to get out of that unpleasant company. One of them had courage left over and followed me down.

So now the fight was equal again. At the same altitude we flew toward one another head on. We approached each other with the great speed of four hundred kilometers an hour. The opponent was a two-seater, I was alone. The Englishman had the advantage in that his observer could shoot at me the moment I flew past him, while I had to first turn around again to fire in the direction of flight with my single-seat fighter. Here you must aim clean, otherwise you will get the worst of it—a thought that went through my head. We were not two hundred meters away from each other; therefore, there was not much time left in which to shoot. On such occasions it often happens that both parties fatally collide. If I do not dispatch the opponent before he is near, we must turn aside at the same time, and then comes the moment when I am at a disadvantage. Of course one shoots as long as possible at the other, hoping that each single bullet one gets off will indeed be enough. At the last moment one pulls the machine up and hopes that the opponent has gone down on one side or the other. On the other hand, if I hit my opponent, I know from experience that he will make an unexpected turn. In such a case it is impossible to know on which side he will turn away. I have had quite a bit of experience shooting down opponents from in front.

We rushed toward each other shooting. At the last moment I noticed I had hit him. A blazing airplane whizzed by me. I pulled my machine around and made such a sharp turn that I was three quarters on my back. A sea of fire in the form of the Englishmen whistled right by me. The observer stood up and stared into the flames. Completely ablaze, the English machine made another turn. Both crewmen jumped out along the way. The rest of the machine fluttered in the air.

This battle went so quickly that I shot down another from the same squadron and helped a third along. I wounded both crewmen of the second. They had to land near us. At about fifty meters the fellow went into a spin with his two-seater and then straightened out to land. Spinning is a dive in which no steering is done. One can also do it deliberately in order to deceive his opponent, who often thinks he is really finished. In this case the pilot would merely have the fun of a long captivity. The crewmen whose airplanes were forced to land by my brother and me said at their interrogation that they had heard of the Richthofen brothers. Neither my brother nor I had ever seen them . . .

THE 21ST OF APRIL 1918

Army Report of 24 April 1918

Rittmeister Freiherr Von Richthofen has not returned from pursuit of an opponent over the Somme battlefield. According to an English report, he has fallen.

To Major Freiherr Von Richthofen . . .

To my great sorrow, I have just received from the Commanding General of the Air Service the report that your brave son, Rittmeister Freiherr Von Richthofen, has fallen. What the youthful leader accomplished in aerial combat will never be forgotten by Me, My army and the German people. I share sincerely in your sorrow. May God grant you the balm of his comfort.

Wilhelm

So often with each report of a victory by your son I have trembled for his life, which he had dedicated to the King and the Fatherland, and now God has ordained that the pride of you and of all of us must come to an end. Your son stands in my mind for his modesty and simple airs, as I had the joy of meeting him in May of last year. I could not deny myself the opportunity to see him soar into the air from the airfield. The

Lord be with you and yours in your great grief. I hope that the condition of your second son is satisfactory.

Victoria

Sadly moved by the report that your son has given up his life for the Fatherland, I express my deepest sympathy to you and your wife. As master of the German flying force, as a model for every German man, he will live on in the memory of the German people. May this be a comfort in your grief.

Von Hindenburg

The Commanding General prepared the following radio message to *Jagdgeschwader* I on the occasion of the death of Rittmeister Manfred Freiherr von Richthofen:

The hope we all cherished, that Richthofen would be saved, was not realized. He has fallen. Stronger than our words are his deeds. It was allowed him to be recognized as a leader, honored in life, and loved as a comrade. We will not turn our gaze to what he could have done, but, rather, we the living will constantly cherish the memory of his deeds. I am sincerely mindful of his *Jagdgeschwader* and especially his *Jagdstaffel* 11.

The Commanding General
/s/ Von Hoeppner

THE LAST BATTLE

BY

Captain A. Roy Brown, R.F.C.

A. Roy Brown,[1] Canadian Captain in the Royal Flying Corps whose bullet killed Manfred von Richthofen, has told the following about his aerial combat with Von Richthofen, in which the German fell:

I had a school friend who was then with me in the same squadron. That was Captain May, and we were both very good friends. On Sunday morning, the twenty-first of April 1918, we were in the air together along with other members of our squadron. On the way home we met a number of enemy fliers. We got into a fight, and I want to say at the outset that after a few seconds I had given up hope of ever coming out of this engagement alive. I looked over at my friend Captain May, and my heart beat with joy despite all my trouble, as I saw that May had succeeded in shooting down a German flier. May immediately turned from his victory to fly home. I had urged him to do that because he was a novice and because he would have gotten tired in the fight, so there was no purpose in his staying in the air long. But the moment he flew off, I saw a red airplane set out after him. I became uncomfortable. As I went to help him, I had to fight for my own life, as three fliers came down to crush me. I was in a crossfire of their guns, with no way out! In any event, I wanted to make it as

---

[1] Although Captain Brown was officially credited with the victory, doubt still exists as to how or by whom Von Richthofen was killed.

unpleasant as possible for them! So I tried to remain calm. I cannot remember having been afraid but only thinking that, should this be the end, it was good that at least it was in the cockpit of my old machine. I began to maneuver. Shots here and there followed in quick succession as I spiraled and zigzagged to offer the smallest target. I tried every trick I knew and some that I had never tried. Finally the thought occurred to me to get them involved in a collision. I let them come straight toward me, then I did an "Immelmann," up, then back. I appeared to come under them. Directly, I could see two of them shoot by within a hair's breadth of each other. The third would almost have been included if he had not made a wide turn.

I had time to catch my breath. While they leveled off, I tried to climb for altitude. Then they turned and came after me again. I held my course until they almost collided with me, then I tipped over on my side and was flatly beneath them. Again they narrowly escaped collision. With all my might I tried to gain altitude. By leveling off, they lost sight of me.

My first thought was: "Where is May?" Anxiously I searched the sky for him, hoping to see him alive. Finally I spotted him north of me, flying home in the direction of Corbie.

He was still being followed. From out of the mist a bright red airplane shot after him in such an advantageous position as to be easily fatal for him. I climbed further up to eventually bring help to May. He tried to get away, turning here and there and zigzagging, but the "red one" stayed steadfastly behind him. They were like two giant hornets hunting one another, forward, sideward, and around again. They made every movement together. Each turn of May's was repeated by his opponent. However, May did not appear to be inferior to him.

Yet I soon saw the German close the gap. He gave up all

maneuvers and flew in a straight line. He cut down the distance noticeably. He now had the advantage if he succeeded in maintaining his pace . . . Suddenly it became clear to me that May was in a trap. He had tried every trick he knew, and now was at his wit's end. The red plane was scarcely a hundred feet away and on the same level of May; any second he could open fire. Luckily, I had meanwhile reached three thousand feet. I swiveled sharply around, turned, leveled off and then, nose down, I shot at the tail of the "red one."

I had all the trump cards in my hand. I was above him and came from behind. May twisted and turned like a fish on a line. The "red one" then brought his first burst of fire to bear when the moment for me had come!

May had given up. "The end," he thought and got ready for the death blow. Then he heard my machine gun. He looked over his shoulder. "Thank God, Brownie!"

As he looked around again, the "red one" had disappeared. Over the edge of his airplane he saw him hit the ground below.

Richthofen's end was exactly like that of most of his victims. He had been surprised, and he was dead before he could recover from his surprise.

Everything had happened so much by chance, so simply. I dove down until I was on his tail, then I fired. The bullets tore into his elevator and mutilated the rear part of the airplane. Flames showed where the bullets struck.

Aimed too short! Quite gradually I pulled on the stick . . . I came up a little, it was like gunnery-school practice. A full burst ripped into the side of the airplane. The pilot turned around and looked back. I saw the glint of his eyes behind the big goggles, then he collapsed in the seat, bullets whistled by him. I ceased firing.

Richthofen was dead. It all happened in seconds, faster than one can tell. His airplane shook, tottered, rolled over and plunged down.

The reserve trenches of the Australians lay only three hundred feet beneath us; it was a short plunge. May saw it, Mellersh saw it, and I did as I swung around.

Mellersh was grazed on the hand. Two enemies were around behind him. I went over as fast as I could to help him. One German spiraled out of the fight and flew off, as did the other. The fight was over, everyone had had enough.

I wearily turned back to Bertangles. The violent maneuvers had badly weakened my plane. However, I managed to reach the aerodrome.

The first to greet me was May. He ran up to me and grabbed my hand. "Thank God, Brown. Did you get the red one? It looked bad. A second later and it would have been all over for me."

He was glad to still be alive. Not a word was mentioned about Richthofen. I also said nothing. I probably had the feeling that every red fighter pilot was Richthofen, the German eagle of the air. However, the thought of having been victorious over him was presumptuous.

Soon thereafter I sat down to write my report. There I mentioned that I had destroyed a bright red machine. My logbook shows under that date the following entry: "Dived on a large formation of enemy machines, Albatros single-seaters. Three machines followed me and I came out. Gained altitude. Turned back and shot at a completely red machine that followed May down. I sent him down. Observed by Lieutenants Mellersh and May, then attacked two fliers that followed Mellersh. Unsuccessful."

Rrrrrr . . . rrrr, the telephone. The Commandant was on the telephone. Simpsons, our chief engineer, went to answer. He came back!

"Man, Brownie! Get ready for a medal!"

"What for?"

"The old man says the red flier was Richthofen."

I almost fainted. Certainly I had already had a feeling he

was the one. But Richthofen! The "Red Baron," Germany's most famous flier!

It was a glorious day in the squadron. Finally we began the meal. We had just finished the last course when Cairns, the Commandant, entered. We saluted, he came over to me and looked down seriously. No willingness to congratulate was noticeable. His voice coolly intoned:

"So, Brown, you claim to have shot Richthofen down?"

"No, by no means!"

"But, I thought."

"No, I claim only to have shot down a red-colored Fokker. I don't know who the pilot was."

"Well, it was Richthofen! But the situation is that the Australian machine-gun section says that they knocked him down. Besides an announcement that he was brought down by an RE 8, and then your report. It looks bad enough!"

Then we got into the car the Commandant had left waiting, and drove to the quarters of the 11th Australian Infantry Brigade. We drove without speaking a word. Cairns did not speak much as it was, and I passed the time talking to the air. We found the infantry Commander's tent well-hidden on a hill in the middle of the wood. I believe it was somewhere west of Corbie.

We found Richthofen. He had been laid down in the vicinity of an aviation field hospital. A few men stood around.

The sight of Richthofen as I walked closer gave me a start. He appeared so small to me, so delicate. He looked so friendly; his feet were slender, like those of a woman. They were set in his Uhlan boots, brightly polished. An elegance emanated from them that was not at all proper as they showed from beneath his coarse flight suit.

His cap had been removed. Blond, silk-soft hair, like that of a child, fell from the broad, high forehead. His face, particularly peaceful, had an expression of gentleness and goodness, of refinement.

Suddenly I felt miserable, desperately unhappy, as if I had committed an injustice. There could be no feeling of joy that there lay Richthofen, the greatest of all! With a feeling of shame, a kind of anger against myself moved in my thoughts, that I had forced him to lay there, so calm, so peaceful, lifeless. This man, who shortly before had been so full of life.

And in my heart I cursed the force that is devoted to death. I gnashed my teeth, I cursed the war!

If I could, I would gladly have brought him back to life, but that was somewhat different than shooting a gun. I could no longer look him in the face.

I went away. I did not feel like a victor. There was a lump in my throat. I waited until Cairns was finished with the inquiry. If he had been my dearest friend, I could not have had greater sorrow. Surely I would not have felt so miserable if I had not had the misfortune of knowing I had killed him.[2]

[2] Several accounts of Von Richthofen's last fight have been written under Captain A. Roy Brown's by-line; however, Brown's actual authorship has long been in question. This particular account appeared in the 1933 edition of Von Richthofen's memoirs and is translated from the German.

19   A captured Albatros D I single-seater similar to the D II
model flown by Von Richthofen *(United States Air Force)*

20   Pfalz D III, a type of aircraft flown by the Red Baron
(United States Air Force)

21   Albatros D V *(United States Air Force)*

22 The great Fokker D VII (*United States Air Force*)

23 Cockpit of the Fokker D VII
(*United States Air Force Museum*)

24   The Fokker Dr I triplane *(National Archives)*

25   Last of the World War I Fokker fighters, the Fokker D VIII *(National Archives)*

26   This is why the Fokker D VIII was known as the "Flying Razor" *(National Archives)*

27   A line-up of Albatros D III fighters, with an Albatros two-seater bringing up the rear *(United States Air Force)*

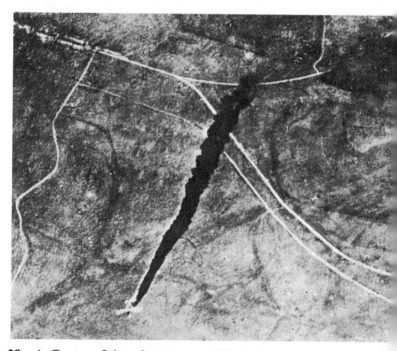

28   A German fighter has sent an Allied plane down in flames *(United States Air Force)*

29 An FE 2b of the type downed by the Baron
(*National Archives*)

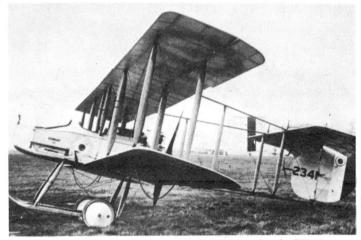

30 A Vickers FB 5 "Gunbus," often mistaken for the FE 2b
(*National Archives*)

31 The BE 2d (*National Archives*)

32 An FE 8 similar to this one fell before Von Richthofen's guns on 23 January 1917 (*National Archives*)

33 The Nieuport 17c (*National Archives*)

34 A line-up of RFC Sopwith 1½ Strutters and their crews (*United States Air Force*)

35 The Spad VII *(United States Air Force)*

36 Von Richthofen claimed a number of RE 8s on his victory list *(National Archives)*

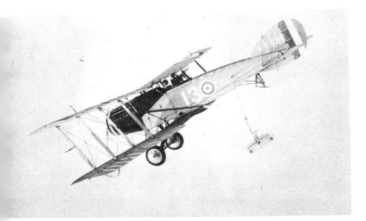

37 The Bristol Fighter known as the "Brisfit." It was one of the few two-seater types designated as a fighter *(United States Air Force)*

38 The SE 5, probably the best World War I fighting machine to emerge from the Royal Aircraft Factory at Farnborough *(United States Air Force)*

39 The famous Sopwith Camel *(United States Air Force)*

40 A formation of Sopwith Camels similar to the one led by Captain A. Roy Brown against which Von Richthofen fought his last battle *(United States Air Force)*

"THE BRAVE AND WORTHY OPPONENT"

The Funeral and Burial of
Rittmeister Manfred Freiherr von Richthofen

The Richthofen family obtained a complete account of the burial of Richthofen from the English and Americans. It follows here:

A high, deep tent was spread out, and in the middle of this tent, on a raised platform, lay the body of Manfred von Richthofen in the uniform of the 1st Uhlans that he wore when black fate plucked away his life. The sides of the linen tent fluttered in the wind, and the light that shone weakly in the tent illuminated his sharply defined, young face.

At five o'clock in the afternoon military detachments gathered near the tent. Twelve English soldiers, steel helmets on their heads, marched under the command of an officer and formed an honor guard in front of the tent. Six English flying officers, all squadron leaders who had been decorated for encounters with the enemy, stepped into the tent and raised the coffin in which the dead man lay to their shoulders. The troops who had been positioned as an honor guard presented arms, and the English fliers carried the dead enemy comrade to a car that was set slowly in motion.

Thus the procession moved to the entrance of a small war cemetery. At the gate stood the English cleric with a surplice over his khaki uniform. The coffin followed the twelve men in the funeral procession, they had their eyes to the ground and carried their rifles reversed. And then came English officers and N.C.O.s. Among them, too, were fifty fliers who were in the vicinity, and they all went silently, with eyes lowered, behind the coffin. The fliers had gathered hurriedly to pay their last respects to the brave and noble enemy. They brought wreaths wound in immortelle and decorated with the German colors. These wreaths now lay on the coffin. But one of the officers carried a great wreath that bore the inscription: "Captain von Richthofen, the brave and worthy foe." This wreath was sent from the Headquarters of the British Royal Air Force.[1]

The cleric delivered the eulogy. Officers, N.C.O.s and men stood around the grave; and, when the cleric had ended, they all stepped back as the sharp command of an English officer called the men of the funeral procession to take up position and raise their rifles into the air. And then the last salute cracked over the grave.

On the coffin was nailed a metal plate that bore the inscription in German and English: "Here rests Captain Manfred Freiherr von Richthofen, fallen on the field of honor at twenty-five years, in an aerial combat on 21 April 1918."

Airplanes bearing the tricolor cockades crossed over the grave as the coffin slowly sank downwards. This grave lies not far from Amiens. A copse of hawthorne that is always lashed by the wind throws its shadow on the city where Manfred von Richthofen was laid down to his last sleep.

[1] The RAF was born on 1 April 1918 with the merger of the Royal Flying Corps and Royal Naval Air Service.

RETURN HOME

BY

Bolko Freiherr von Richthofen

At Home

In the middle of the year 1925 our family decided to transfer the mortal remains of Manfred von Richthofen to Germany and to inter him in his native soil. At first it was intended to place Manfred's coffin next to the grave of his father and his brother Lothar in the Schweidnitz Cemetery. But the authorities of the German Republic—above all, the Defense Ministry and the fliers' organizations—declared the earnest wish to have the last resting place for Manfred's body in the Invaliden Cemetery in Berlin, in which so many German heroes and field commanders have found their eternal rest. The family agreed to this in the knowledge that the remembrance and memory of Manfred were not theirs alone, but, rather, belonged to the entire German people. The necessary and time-consuming negotiations with the French authorities were got underway, and in the middle of November I traveled to France to the site of Manfred's grave. This was not the original place, because after the war his body was brought to Fricourt, a small village eight kilometers from the once hotly contested village of Albert, where there was a German soldiers' cemetery.

The proper authorities assigned to me a gentleman named Lienhard, who was to settle the necessary formalities with the

French courts and the administration of exhumation. It was on the fourteenth of November 1925 when I came from Amiens to Albert to meet Monsieur Lienhard. I found this very prudent and zealous gentleman somewhat excited, as the French authorities, although they had been informed of the exhumation in good time, had unfortunately done nothing to its end. After some inquiries, we succeeded in finding an old gentleman who had been an N.C.O. in the war and now held the position of cemetery caretaker. We took him with us in our car and went directly to Fricourt. The German soldiers' cemetery there offered a truly stirring picture, and the impression I got from the view is hard to put into words. According to the statement of the caretaker accompanying us, about six thousand German soldiers lay there in single graves and about twelve thousand in one immense mass grave. There was not a sprouting leaf, much less any kind of wreath, to give this sad and deeply moving place a somewhat friendly feeling. Only on the mass grave there lay a plain metal wreath that perhaps an old mother had dedicated to the memory of her son who rested there with thousands of his comrades who had fallen for the fatherland. In the first years after the war the bodies of the German heroes were gathered here from thirty different cemeteries. Of course, location in the cemetery was not final at the time. Meanwhile, the Association for the Care of German War Graves also took this resting place for dead combatants into its care, and today it hopefully offers a friendlier and prettier view.

The cemetery at Fricourt was also not ready yet for the exhumation. We had to bring every single worker there, and it took almost three hours before the excavation itself could be made. We found a zinc plate on which was recorded Manfred's name and date of death in English and German. In its time this plate had been placed by the English on his coffin at the first interment. Now it is in the possession of my mother in Schweidnitz. After the transfer of all that remained of

Manfred to a zinc coffin we had brought with us, we then brought it to Albert, where it was loaded onto a train going to Kehl, on the German-French border, under the direction of the proper French authorities.

It was on Monday, the sixteenth of November, at midnight, when a French locomotive with only a coal tender and a freight car rolled slowly across the Rhine bridge at Kehl. Whistle signals sounded shrilly, and as the small train entered the station the few trainmen on duty took their caps off. Manfred's mortal remains had come home. The next morning the coffin case made of rough boards was lifted into a luggage car of the German Railway System and laid out there under pine rings and flowers. All of Tuesday passed with negotiations between German authorities in Kehl and the French Occupation Commandant, who decided not to give approval to a patriotic ceremony at Manfred's coffin in the train station. But he had indeed not quite rightly estimated the intentions of his superiors, and in the evening hours the Occupation Command gave approval to hold a suitable ceremony. All the bells of the small Baden city began to sound, alarming the fire brigade. And so the whole population, from the oldest man to the youngest child who could walk, came to respectfully greet Manfred's body on German soil. On Wednesday at six o'clock in the morning the car was taken from Kehl to Appenweier, and there it was coupled to the regularly scheduled Frankfurt express train. From then until it reached Berlin, Manfred's last journey turned out to be a triumphal procession through Germany's most beautiful provinces, the like of which had scarcely ever been seen. Everywhere the bells in the towns and villages sounded, flags dipped, airplanes accompanied the train, and the wish of the populace was followed in leaving open the doors of the baggage car in which fighter pilots of the old army held a death watch, so that the masses of waiting men, women and children standing on the banks of the rail line could at least see the coffin. When the train stopped—in Baden-Oos, Rastatt, Karlsruhe, Durlach, Bruchsal, Heidelberg—patriotic songs greeted the coffin. And there was no difference between parties and groups that appeared. Veterans' groups, officers' organizations, the Jewish Front Soldiers' Club, the Escherich Organization, the Werewolf, the Order of Young Germans, the *Stahlhelm,* and as many others as there are names for, all appeared in rare harmony to honor the homecoming dead hero. The wreaths were heaped in mountains, and between them lay small bouquets and single flowers; for even those who could only spend a few pennies took it upon themselves to show their thankfulness and respect for the great fighter pilot. Clearly, we who escorted Manfred's body felt that the people had understood that his trip home to the fatherland had symbolic significance. Not all of the hundreds of thousands who gave their lives for Germany and who found their last resting places in foreign soil could travel home. And so we wanted the greeting of our dead Manfred by the assembled masses of the people to be the symbol of the sacrificed German heroes, and to honor in him the sons and brothers who had given up their lives to the fatherland.

On Wednesday, the eighteenth of November, the train pulled into Berlin shortly after ten o'clock at night. At the Potsdam train station a ceremonial reception took place in which deputies from the Ring of the Fliers and the traditional company were represented. Members of the 1st Uhlan Regiment, in which Manfred had served, carried the coffin to the hearse that took him to the *Gnadenkirche* [Church of Mercy] in the *Invalidenstrasse*. At *Potsdamer Platz* the police had to set up a barricade. A large crowd of mourners had gathered there; they were silent and bareheaded as the funeral procession passed. On Thursday morning the body lay in state in the *Gnadenkirche*. Now the zinc coffin was placed in a brown oak casket, Uhlan swords and *tschapkas* lay on the coffin. In front of the coffin stood the wooden cross that had marked

Manfred's grave in Fricourt. It bore only his name and the number 53091. The honor guard included men who had been officers in his *Jagdgeschwader* and in the 1st Uhlan Regiment. In unbroken succession Berlin's population filed past the coffin the whole day.

On the afternoon of the twentieth of November the interment took place. At noon the procession of the mass of people began. Then came President Von Hindenburg, who greeted my mother and me. With him appeared Chancellor Luther, General Von Seeckt at the head of the Berlin generals, and Admiral Zenker with the officers of the Navy. The ceremony at the church was short and dignified. Then eight fliers, all knights of the order of the *Pour le mérite,* raised the coffin to the gun carriage of the 2nd Prussian Artillery Regiment. A company of the sentry regiment was set at the head, and with muffled drums the procession went by streets lined with countless organizations to the Invaliden Cemetery. An earlier regimental comrade who was now a member of the *Reichswehr* carried before the coffin the cushion bearing the decorations that had been presented to Manfred during his lifetime. Above the cemetery airplanes crossed with black pennants, and the honor guard fired the last salute three times. While the *Reichswehr* chorus sang the "Song of Good Comrades," the coffin sank down. The Minister of the *Reichswehr* spoke these words:

"When we give Manfred von Richthofen's mortal remains back to the earth, at the same time we take the solemn vow that we belong in faith and hope to our fatherland, for which he fell."

Among the countless participants of this sad ceremony there was no one who did not agree with these words in the innermost part of his soul. Thus, Manfred found his last, enduring resting place in the middle of the Reich's capital. But how much his memory lives on in the hearts of the people is shown by the thousands and thousands of countrymen who, year in and year out, above all on Sundays and holidays, visit his grave in great numbers, sadly and thoughtfully, but at the same time filled with patriotic pride, kneeling in spirit before the name of the knightly German hero of the air.

MY BROTHER MANFRED

BY

Bolko Freiherr von Richthofen

Even if he is allotted a long life, a man will always remain to a certain degree a product of his origin and upbringing. But when called away early from earthly existence, the inheritance of his parents and ancestors and the impressions of his childhood and youth will be found to have played a major role in the shaping of a man's deeds and actions. And so it was with my beloved brother, Manfred Freiherr von Richthofen; for before he had completed his twenty-sixth year of life he met a hero's death. Whoever would tell the story of his life must go back to the history and manner of the family from which he was descended, and must depict the surroundings and the people with whom he grew up, and those observations current to him. These contributed to the development of his character and enabled him in his youth to perform extraordinarily for the people and the fatherland.

The Richthofen family originated in Bernau in the Brandenburg Marches that were once larger than Berlin. Bernau is now only a small neighboring city of the capital. In that place, Sebastian Schmidt, born in Koblenz and once a pupil of Luther's in Wittenberg, was the Lutheran deacon from 1543 to 1553. According to the custom of the time and because of his spiritual calling, he Latinized his name and called himself "Faber." The family originated with him and his wife, Barbara Below, the daughter of a town councilor from Berlin.

But it presumably would never have taken a more than usual rise in fortune if Pastor Faber had not become a casual friend of a man his own age who was judged to be the most prominent man in the Margravate of Brandenburg. This was Paulus Schultze, or Schultheiss, who was descended from the Schultze family of Bernau and whose father and grandfather, Andreas and Thomas Schultze, became *Bürgermeisters* of Bernau about the beginning of the sixteenth century. Paulus Schultze also Latinized his name, and so he is called "Paulus Praetorius" in the history of the Brandenburg Marches.

Paulus Praetorius was born in Bernau on 24 January 1521, and died in Moritzburg near Halle on 16 June 1565 as Imperial and Electoral Counsel of Brandenburg, Archbishop of Magdeburg and Privy Counselor of the Exchequer of Halberstadt, and Fiefmaster and Magistrate of different estates which had been acquired during his relatively short life. Under all pictures of him are found the words, *Vir prudens et orator gravissimus,* which translate, A prudent man and distinguished speaker. And truly this Paulus Praetorius must have been an important learned gentleman. Indeed, in his early years he was appointed an instructor to the Margraves Friedrich and Sigismund of Brandenburg, the sons of Elector Joachim II, who both later became Archbishops of Magdeburg. He won the highest confidence of his electoral master, into whose intimate counsel he was appointed and who sent him on different diplomatic missions, especially to the imperial court in Prague, to Ferdinand, the Holy Roman Emperor. So it was that the same Emperor Ferdinand I Oculi in 1566 presented him and his heirs a noble coat of arms that appropriately represented Praetorius as a Praetor, i.e., one who sits on a tribunal, a black-robed judge.

But Paulus Praetorius had no male heirs; so he decided in 1543 to adopt the son of his friend Sebastian Faber in Bernau, Samuel Faber, or, as he was called after that, Samuel Praetorius. Samuel survived Paulus Praetorius in not only his newly gained coat of arms, but also in his obviously important properties. Samuel Praetorius was also a learned man. He moved to Frankfurt on the Oder and was a town councilor, recorder, and finally *Bürgermeister*. He died there in 1605. His son Tobias Praetorius (1576–1644) enlarged the family fortune and acquired the first property in Silesia through his marriage to a noblewoman. He also turned more and more from the circle of learned patricians to that of the landed gentry. His son Johann Praetorius (1611–64) moved to Silesia and in 1661 was advanced by Kaiser Leopold I to hereditary Bohemian knighthood with the addition of the surname Von Richthofen. The Richthofen family that flourishes today is derived from Johann Praetorius von Richthofen.

From the middle of the seventeenth century this family has been prominent in Silesia, especially in the Streigau, Tauer, Schweidnitz and Liegnitz circle, and remains so to this day. The Holy Roman Emperor in Vienna was so grateful for their lasting help and consideration that the family from the Brandenburg Marches lived on. And, about one hundred years later, when Frederick the Great made Silesia a Prussian province, every member of the family, without exception, joined the new ruling house (which was really quite old to them). Frederick the Great rewarded this support on 6 November 1741 with the elevation of the family to the baronial ranks of the Kingdom of Prussia.

The vast majority of the Richthofen family have remained engaged in agriculture ever since the days the first Silesian property was acquired. Generations have devoted themselves to the management and maintenance of the extensive estates, although public welfare, through the activity of the Silesian provincial government, has not been overlooked. In war and peace the generations of the family have done their obvious duty for the defense of the province and the kingdom. General of the Cavalry, Manfred von Richthofen, the godfather of my brother, led an army in the World War.

But the inclination toward learned professions had by no means disappeared with the descendants of the town-councilors, pastors, and *Bürgermeisters*. And the example of the adopted father Paulus Praetorius led many members of the family into political and diplomatic professions. Moreover, a familiar name to lawyers today is that of German law theoretician and professor of the University of Berlin, Karl Freiherr von Richthofen, a specialist in the area of Old Germanic and especially Frisian laws. And Ferdinand von Richthofen's great reputation as one of the first geographers, not only of Germany but of the world, remains unchanged. Even now, almost thirty years after his death, the name of this unequaled China scholar lives on today in the mountains and rivers visited by him and named after him.

In the political formation of our fatherland right up to recent times a multitude of family members have had important influence. Oswald Freiherr von Richthofen was the Prussian Minister of State and State Secretary of the Foreign Office of long standing during the chancellorship of Prince Bülow, and the Freiherrn Karl, Ernst, Hartmann and Praetorius von Richthofen were in the National Assembly at Weimar, both before and after the Republic.

The separation of our family came during the early part of the eighteenth century. Our closest relatives in the other branch have not distinguished themselves, but our immediate forebears established the estates we now hold. Their wives came predominantly from the Silesian nobility, such as the Von Reibnitz, Von Heintze-Weissenrode, and Von Lüttwitz families. Our great-grandmother was born Thecla von Berenhorst in Dessau in 1808. She was a granddaughter of the Prussian Field Marshal Prince Leopold von Anhalt-Dessau, the famous old man of Dessau. Her father, Georg Heinrich von Berenhorst, ducal Lord High Steward of Anhalt-Dessau, was descended from a union between Prince Leopold and a young commoner. If one will, one could perhaps assume that the blood of the victor of Höchstädt, Turin and Kesselsdorf was effectively unchanged in his descendants. Our grandmother's maiden name is Marie Seip. She was descended from a Mecklenburg landowner family of Hessian origin which stood as close as relatives to the Goethe family. We grandchildren loved our grandmother very much. She died before the outbreak of the World War. Vacation visits to the *Gute Romberg* with our grandparents are among the wonderful memories of our youth. At the beginning of vacation grandmother welcomed us as we set foot in the old shingle house, with the encouraging words, "Here you can do what you want." We boys did not need to have that said twice, and the joys of country life—riding, hunting, swimming, and everything that belongs to it—were thoroughly enjoyed.

Our father, Albrecht Freiherr von Richthofen, born in 1859, was the first active officer of our lineage and served in the Prince's own dragoon regiment in Breslau. Both my brothers were born there also—Manfred in 1892 and Lothar in 1894. Father, a major, had to quit the service relatively early because an ear disease made a further military career impossible to him. He once leaped from a bridge into a river in full uniform to save one of his dragoons from drowning. The dragoon had fallen off his horse while crossing the Oder. The cold that father caught in so doing unfortunately led to his retirement from the Army due to a hearing difficulty. During the World War he was active as a local commandant of a small city in the vicinity of Lille, near Manfred's squadron. He went to his eternal rest in 1920 in Schweidnitz, where he and my mother had gone in retirement and where my mother lives today as the keeper and caretaker of the mementos of her fallen sons. She has made her house in Schweidnitz a place for the memory of Manfred von Richthofen.

Our mother, born in 1868, comes from the families of Schickfuss and Neudorff, owning large estates in Silesia. Her mother, born a Von Falkenhausen, stems from a very well-known military family whose ancestor, Margrave Karl Wilhelm Friedrich von Ansbach, is descended from the extinct Frankish lineage of the house of Hohenzollern and married a sister of Frederick the Great.

My brothers Manfred and Lothar were eleven and nine years older, respectively, than I, and so my reminiscences of them begin shortly before both of them entered the Army. But my parents have told me so much about their early youth, especially Manfred's, that, with no risk of reporting falsely, I am in a position to add to the story of his childhood and youth.

It was always a great joy to my parents that from Manfred's first days he had an especially robust and healthy nature. He was really sick only once in his life, with the measles, and he deeply regretted that because he had never before missed a school day. Manfred had a marvelously fit body. Even as a small boy he turned somersaults without using his hands. He held them along the seams of his trousers, rigid as a soldier. At eight years of age he scaled the highest apple tree on the property, one that no one else could reach. And then he did not lower himself down the trunk but, rather, with the greatest dexterity caught hold of a branch and swung down. My parents often saw him do this, but never had the feeling that anything would happen, because he was so sure of all his movements. My mother, especially, had never been uneasy with us boys. She was of the opinion that children could grow fit only when one allowed them freedom of movement. Only when exposed to a wide variety of physical dangers could they mature so as to be able to judge what they themselves were capable of. Their exploits were not always without incident, but nothing serious ever happened. Only once did Manfred cause my parents concern. He suffered a serious knee wound while in the Cadet Corps. A piece of cartilage in the knee was pulled away as he dropped into a squatting position. The piece pinched off a nerve beneath the kneecap, so the leg tottered at the side. Massage as well as all sorts of warm baths did not help, and for a year the leg remained unimproved. My mother was especially depressed. Trying to console my parents, Manfred said: "When I can no longer run on my legs, I will walk on my hands." And, as if completely healthy, he walked through the room on his hands with both legs extended into the air. After that it was decided at last that he should have an operation. Happily, this turned out well, and in a few weeks he was fully restored to health again.

When Manfred became a cadet officer in Uhlan Regiment 1, "Kaiser Alexander III," he resumed the passion for horses he had before his injury. After he received his commission as an officer, our father bought him a beautiful mare. Manfred praised this horse to me as a truly remarkable animal, almost indestructible. She went through her paces like a lamb, and although quite gentle, jumped a meter and sixty. Manfred won many beautiful trophies with her in jumping and hurdles competition. With another horse he won the Kaiser Prize Race in 1913. This was the climax of his racing ambitions, which had led him to the great races in Breslau and the capital, Berlin. To this end he acquired a thoroughbred named Antithesis. But on the day he was to have ridden this horse in its first race, he was riding him across the Russian border. But he had ridden many horses to victory in many other races.

Manfred put an unusual amount of energy into whatever he did from the days of his youth. As an eight-year-old boy in Breslau he was to have waited for my parents at the train station. He was returning from a long visit in the country and had with him two large bags containing his clothing. A boy was sent to the train station to fetch Manfred, but he returned alone. Manfred was not to be found. What had happened? They had no telephones then. The tension mounted. While my parents deliberated what to do, the doorbell rang and there stood Manfred at the door, safe and sound with both bags.

"You should have taken a carriage."

"No, I had no money."

"Who carried the bags for you?"

"I did."

My parents were speechless and doubtful that the boy had been able to lift them, as they were so heavy. But then Manfred explained, "I could lift one of them, so I carried it a ways and then went back for the second, which I fetched past the place I left the first. Unfortunately, it took a long time to get here."

He told his story with such obvious calm and security that my parents were comforted and forgot the anguish he had caused them.

Manfred endured the cadet period, although he did not find this manner of education and management of boys at all promising. But he gritted his teeth and never complained to anyone at the vacation home of our parents. We used to tease him about the school at Wahlstatt, and he would reply that we might not think grammar school was much fun, but it was easier and much better than military school. Nevertheless, Manfred decided very early to prepare for an officer's career, and once the decision was reached, he set out to make that career an exceptional one. At the time he wanted, above all, to become a great cavalry general. Never would he have suspected that his fame would not come of his service as an earthbound soldier, but rather as a warrior of the air. Later when he changed over to the aviation branch in May of 1915, he answered my question as to why he had done it with the words: "I could not devote myself to being only an observer [the main role of the cavalryman in World War I]. I want to be a pilot, and, if so lucky, I want to be the best of them all." And with that, his blue eyes shone and gave proof of the ambition that lived in him.

Manfred was extremely truthful. Even today my mother cannot praise enough the extent to which they, as parents,

could constantly rely on him. He gave precise and clear an-
swers to every question, without regard for what the con-
sequences to himself could be. Once at my grandmother's
estate, as a twelve-year-old boy, he could not curb his passion
for hunting. When he could not find wild ducks in the field,
he killed some domestic ones from grandmother's coop. Manfred was questioned closely, but that lasted only half a minute. He had no thought at all of denying or glossing over his
deed. And dear grandmother gladly forgave with all her
heart her grandson who would not lie. This first "hunting
trophy" of Manfred's, three pin-feathers, hangs today in his
room in Schweidnitz. Manfred gave his mother the blessed
knowledge that she could have confidence in him. Even today
my mother cherishes the sentiments and beliefs of the type
of person Manfred was, summarized in the words: "He stood
firm wherever he was."

This belief in his own ability, coupled with an inner
strength and obvious modesty, I believe, truly made him a
leader to a special degree. His Uhlans, when he was a lieutenant, and later all of his subordinates in the *Jagdgeschwader*
Richthofen, had unshakable faith in him. He did not flatter
them, but he defended them and kept his word, and service
under him was made easier through his cheerfulness and
brightness; indeed, they often thrived on the high spirits he
showed in the face of the most difficult tasks. In the bravery
of his spirit, in his absolute lack of fear, he was an example
to all who followed him in war. Indeed, despite the complete
impossibility of it all, he could demonstrate a new aerial
procedure or undertake an unpleasant task that would have
given anyone else a feeling of anxiety.

He underrated risk, and fear played no role in his life, even
in his earliest youth. The girls believed that the estate house
was supposed to be haunted. A servant had hanged himself
in the attic, and since then his ghost walked about up there,
or so it was told in the servants' quarters. Manfred, then

thirteen, wanted to see this ghost. He was shown the exact place in the attic where the unfortunate event had happened and he brought up his bed to sleep there. My mother knew of Manfred's fearlessness, but she decided to put it to the test. She crept upstairs with my sister and began to roll chestnuts along the floor. At first Manfred was fast asleep. But as the din increased, he awoke, jumped up, grabbed a club and pounced on the disturbers. My mother had to put on a light so that harm would not come to her. But there was no trace of anxiety in Manfred. And this fearlessness remained with him right up to his last flight.

Manfred went up in the air many hundreds of times, often three or four times in the same day. He knew well that everyone had an Achilles heel and that he also was vulnerable. But of all the men who went through the war with him, there is not one who, anytime he prepared to fly against the enemy, noticed anything other than assurance of victory and belief in himself and success. Perhaps at first Manfred's ambition and love of sport were the motives for his decision to move up from the saddle to the cockpit of his world-famous red fighter plane. But the harder and more difficult the battles became, and the more meaningful the air battle for Germany's destiny, the greater was Manfred's own sense of responsibility. With it all came the clearness and confidence of the spirit of his unbending will to give his best for the people and for Germany. And the *dulce et decorum est pro patria mori* that his teachers once preached to him, though not always to his joy, in Latin studies and in the Cadet Corps, became the meaning of the short life of combat that was allotted to him from 1915 to 1918.

APPENDIX

VON RICHTHOFEN'S VICTORIES

1916

No.	Date	Place	Type Aircraft Brought Down
1	17 Sept.	near Cambrai	FE 2b
2	23 Sept.	Somme River	Martinsyde G 100
3	30 Sept.	Fremicourt	FE 2b
4	7 Oct.	Equancourt	BE 12
5	10 Oct.	Ypres	BE 12
6	16 Oct.[1]	near Ypres	BE 12
7	3 Nov.	Loupart Wood	FE 2b
8	9 Nov.	Beugny	BE 2c
9	20 Nov.	Geudecourt	BE 12
10	20 Nov.	Grandecourt	FE 2b
11	23 Nov.	Bapaume	DH 2
12	11 Dec.	Mercatel	DH 2
13	20 Dec.	Monchy-le-Preux	DH 2
14	20 Dec.	Moreuil	FE 2b
15	27 Dec.	Ficheux	FE 2b

[1] A discrepancy exists here. 25 Oct. is also given as the date.

1917

No.	Date	Place	Type Aircraft Brought Down
16	4 Jan.	Metz-en-Coutre	Sopwith Pup
17	23 Jan.	Lens	FE 8
18	24 Jan.	Vitry	FE 2b
19	1 Feb.	Thelus	BE 2e
20	14 Feb.	Loos	BE 2d
21	14 Feb.	Mazingarbe	BE 2d
22	4 Mar.	Acheville	Sopwith 1½ Strutter
23	4 Mar.	Loos	BE 2d
24	3 Mar.	Souchez	BE 2c
25	9 Mar.	Bailleul	DH 2
26	11 Mar.	Vimy	BE 2d
27	17 Mar.	Oppy	FE 2b
28	17 Mar.	Vimy	BE 2c
29	21 Mar.	La Neuville	BE 2c
30	24 Mar.	Givenchy	Spad VII
31	25 Mar.	Tilloy	Nieuport 17
32	2 Apr.	Farbus	BE 2d
33	2 Apr.	Givenchy	Sopwith 1½ Strutter
34	3 Apr.	Lens	FE 2d
35	5 Apr.	Lembras	Bristol Fighter F 2a
36	5 Apr.	Quincy	Bristol Fighter F 2a
37	7 Apr.	Mercatel	Nieuport 17
38	8 Apr.	Farbus	Sopwith 1½ Strutter
39	8 Apr.	Vimy	BE 2e
40	11 Apr.	Willerval	BE 2c
41	13 Apr.	Vitry	RE 8
42	13 Apr.	Monchy	FE 2b
43	13 Apr.	Henin	FE 2b
44	14 Apr.	Bois Bernard	Nieuport 17
45	16 Apr.	Bailleul	BE 2c

No.	Date	Place	Type Aircraft Brought Down
46	22 Apr.	Lagnicourt	FE 2b
47	23 Apr.	Mericourt	BE 2e
48	28 Apr.	Pelves	BE 2e
49	29 Apr.	Lecluse	Spad VII
50	29 Apr.	Inchy	FE 2b
51	29 Apr.	Roeux	BE 2d
52	29 Apr.	Billy-Montigny	Nieuport 17
53	18 June	Strugwe	RE 8
54	23 June	Ypres	Spad VII
55	26 June[1]	Keilbergmelen	RE 8
56	25 June	Le Bizet	RE 8
57	2 July	Deulemont	RE 8
58	16 Aug.	Houthulster Wald	Nieuport 17
59	26 Aug.	Poelcapelle	Spad VII
60	2 Sept.	Zonnebeke	RE 8
61	3 Sept.	Bousbecque	Sopwith Pup
62	23 Nov.	Bourlon Wood	DH 5
63	30 Nov.	Moevres	SE 5a

1918

No.	Date	Place	Type Aircraft Brought Down
64	12 Mar.	Nauroy	Bristol Fighter F 2b
65	13 Mar.	Gonnelieu	Sopwith Camel
66	18 Mar.	Andigny	Sopwith Camel
67	24 Mar.	Combles	SE 5a
68	25 Mar.	Contalmaison	Sopwith Camel
69	26 Mar.	Contalmaison	Sopwith Camel
70	26 Mar.	Albert	RE 8
71	27 Mar.	Aveluy	Sopwith Camel
72	27 Mar.	Foucacourt	Bristol Fighter F 2b
73	27 Mar.	Chuignolles	Bristol Fighter F 2b
74	28 Mar.	Mericourt	Armstrong Whitworth FK 8
75	2 Apr.	Moreuil	RE 8

[1] Listed in order of confirmation

No.	Date	Place	Type Aircraft Brought Down
76	6 Apr.	Villers-Bretonneux	Sopwith Camel
77	7 Apr.	Hangard	SE 5a
78	7 Apr.	Villers-Bretonneux	Spad VII
79	20 Apr.	Bois-de-Hamel	Sopwith Camel
80	20 Apr.	Villers-Bretonneux	Sopwith Camel

VON RICHTHOFEN'S DECORATIONS AND AWARDS

German
> Pour le Mérite (The "Blue Max")
> Iron Cross, First Class
> Iron Cross, Second Class
> Order of the House of Hohenzollern
> Order of the Royal House of Oldenburg
> Saxony Military Order of St. Henry
> Griffon Cross
> Hessen Order of Phillips
> Saxe-Coburg-Gotha Duke Karl Edward Medal
> Lippe Schaumberg Cross
> Bremen Hanseatic Cross
> Lübeck Hanseatic Cross

Austro-Hungarian
> Order of the Holy Crown
> Imperial Order of the Iron Crown
> Military Service Cross

Bulgarian
> Order of Military Valor

Turkish
> Star of Gallipoli
> Imtjaz Medal
> Liakat Medal

THE TOP GERMAN ACES, 1914–18

Heading the list of more than 300 German aces was *Rittmeister* Manfred von Richthofen, also known as the "Red Baron" because of his all-red Fokker and Albatros fighters. He was leader of the famous "Flying Circus" and was the ranking ace of both sides—friend and foe—in the First World War.

	Victories
Rittmeister Manfred *Frhr.* von Richthofen	80
Oberleutnant Ernst Udet	62
Oberleutnant Erich Loewenhardt	53
Leutnant Werner Voss	48
Leutnant Fritz Rumey	45
Hauptmann Rudolph Berthold	44
Leutnant Paul Bäumer	43
Leutnant Josef Jacobs	41
Hauptmann Bruno Loerzer	41
Hauptmann Oswald Boelcke	40
Leutnant Franz Büchner	40
Oberleutnant Lothar *Frhr.* von Richthofen	40
Leutnant Karl Menckhoff	39
Leutnant Heinrich Gontermann	39
Leutnant Max Müller	36
Leutnant Julius Buckler	35
Leutnant Gustav Dörr	35
Hauptmann Eduard *Ritter* von Schleich	35
Leutnant Josef Veltjens	34
Leutnant Otto Koennecke	33
Oberleutnant Kurt Wolff	33
Leutnant Heinrich Bongartz	33
Leutnant Theo Osterkamp	32
Leutnant Emil Thuy	32
Leutnant Paul Billik	31

Victories

Rittmeister Karl Bolle	31
Oberleutnant Gotthard Sachsenberg	31
Leutnant Karl Allmenröder	30
Leutnant Karl Degelow	30
Leutnant Heinrich Kroll	30
Leutnant Josef Mai	30
Leutnant Ulrich Neckel	30
Leutnant Karl Schäfer	30
Leutnant Hermann Frommerz	29
Leutnant Walter von Bülow	28
Leutnant Walter Blume	28
Oberleutnant Fritz *Ritter* von Röth	28
Oberleutnant Fritz Bernert	27
Vizefeldwebel Otto Fruhner	27
Leutnant Hans Kirschstein	27
Leutnant Karl Thom	27
Hauptmann Adolf *Ritter* von Tutschek	27
Leutnant Kurt Wüsthoff	27
Oberleutnant Harald Auffahrt	26
Oberleutnant Oscar *Frhr.* von Boenigk	26
Oberleutnant Eduard Dostler	26
Leutnant Arthur Laumann	26
Leutnant Oliver *Frhr.* von Beaulieu-Marconnay	25
Oberleutnant Robert *Ritter* von Greim	25
Leutnant Georg von Hantelmann	25
Leutnant Max Näther	25
Leutnant Fritz Pütter	25
Leutnant Erwin Böhme	24
Leutnant Hermann Becker	23
Leutnant Georg Meyer	23
Oberleutnant Hermann Göring	22
Leutnant Hans Klein	22
Leutnant Hans Pippart	22
Leutnant Werner Preuss	22
Vizefeldwebel Karl Schlegel	22
Leutnant Rudolph Windisch	22

Leutnant Hans Adam	21
Oberleutnant Friedrich Christiansen	21
Leutnant Fritz Friedrichs	21
Leutnant Fritz Höhn	21
Vizefeldwebel Friedrich Altemeier	20
Oberleutnant Hans Bethge	20
Leutnant Rudolph von Eschwege	20
Leutnant Walter Goettsch	20
Leutnant Friedrich Noltenius	20
Hauptmann Wilhelm Reinhard	20

LEADING AUSTRO-HUNGARIAN ACES 1914–18

Like the British, the Austro-Hungarians, Germany's allies, considered only those with ten or more victories as aces. However, some thirty of their pilots downed more than five enemy aircraft apiece.

	Victories
Haupt. Godwin Brumowski	40
Lt. Julius Arigi	32
Lt. Frank Linke-Crawford	30
Lt. Benno Fiala	29
Lt. Josef Kiss	19

LEADING ALLIED ACES, 1914–18

FRENCH

There were a total of 160 aces in the French Aviation Service. Following are those who head the list:

	Victories
Capt. René Fonck	75
Capt. Georges Guynemer	53
Lt. Charles Nungesser	45
Lt. Georges Madon	41
Lt. Maurice Boyeau	35

BRITISH

Some 550 British fighter pilots, including Commonwealth nations (Canada, Australia, New Zealand, Ireland, South Africa, etc.) downed five enemy aircraft each to qualify as aces. There were also nineteen Americans in their ranks. (Officially, the British did not recognize the designation "ace," and in fact considered ten victories as the minimum.)

These are the top five:

	Victories
Maj. Edward "Mick" Mannock	73
Lt. Col. William A. Bishop	72
Maj. Raymond Collishaw	60
Capt. James T. B. McCudden	57
Capt. A. Beauchamp-Proctor	54

BELGIAN

Tiny Belgium produced a total of five aces:

	Victories
Lt. Willy Coppens	34
Lt. Edmond Thieffry	10
Adj. André de Meulemeester	10
Capt. F. Jacquet	7
Lt. Jan Olieslagers	6

AMERICAN

A total of 117 Americans shot down five or more enemy aircraft, officially confirmed, to become aces. Twenty-two of them accomplished this feat while serving exclusively with their British and French Allies. This list includes the top five, and only those who served at some time in the U. S. Air Service.

	Victories
Capt. Edward V. Rickenbacker	26
2nd Lt. Frank Luke, Jr.	21
Maj. Raoul Lufbery	17
1st Lt. George A. Vaughn	13
Capt. Field E. Kindley	12

ITALIAN

Among the 43 Italian fliers who qualified as aces were:

	Victories
Maj. Francesco Baracca	36
Lt. Silvio Scaroni	26

Maj. Pier Ruggiero Piccio	24
Lt. Flavio Barracchini	21
Capt. Fulco Ruffo di Calabria	20

RUSSIAN

Because of the Russian Revolution and the loss and destruction of official records, the total number of Russian aces will never be known. The following five head the list of those whose records remained or were reconstructed.

	Victories
Capt. Alexander Kazakov	17
Capt. P. d'Argueeff	15
Lt. Cmdr. Alexander de Seversky	13
Lt. I. Smirnoff	12
Lt. M. Safonov	11

TYPES OF AIRCRAFT FLOWN BY VON RICHTHOFEN AND/OR HIS *JAGDGESCHWADER*

Two-seaters
  Albatros C I
  Albatros C III

Single-seaters
  Albatros D II
  Albatros D III
  Albatros D V and D Va
  Fokker E I
  Fokker E II
  Fokker E III
  Fokker E IV
  Fokker D III
  Fokker D VII
  Fokker D VIII
  Fokker Dr I Triplane
  Halberstadt D II
  Pfalz D III
  Pfalz Dr I Triplane

TYPES OF AIRCRAFT BROUGHT DOWN
BY VON RICHTHOFEN

Among the Red Baron's eighty victories there were twenty different types and/or models of British and French aircraft. Von Richthofen's first confirmed victory was against an FE 2b. He also shot down more of this type than any other aircraft (unless the three models of BE 2s are combined to give a total destroyed of fourteen). The RE 8 (or "Harry Tate," as it was called by British fliers) was next by weight of numbers among Von Richthofen's victims. The Baron downed eight of them as well as an equal number of Sopwith Camels. His last victory was against a Camel, and it was a Camel that ended Von Richthofen's life. [Although there is some doubt as to who shot him down, official credit was given to Captain A. Roy Brown, a Canadian flying with the Royal Flying Corps (R.F.C.), whose aircraft was a Sopwith Camel.]

The numbers in parentheses following the aircraft name or designation indicate which of Von Richthofen's victories it was, in chronological order. (For example, his first and third victories were scored against Fe 2bs, and his second against a Martinsyde G 100.)

Fe 2b   (1, 3, 7, 10, 14, 15, 18, 27, 42, 43, 46, 50)
Martinsyde G 100   (2)
BE 12c   (4, 5, 6, 9, 24)
BE 2c   (8, 28, 29, 40, 45)
DH 2   (11, 12, 13, 25)
Sopwith Pup   (16, 61)
FE 8   (17)
BE 2e   (19, 39, 47, 48)
BE 2d   (20, 21, 23, 26, 32, 51)
Sopwith 1½ Strutter   (22, 33, 38)
Spad VII   (30, 49, 54, 59, 78)
Nieuport 17   (31, 37, 44, 52, 58)

FE 2d   (34)
Bristol Fighter F 2a   (35, 36)
RE 8   (41, 53, 55, 56, 57, 60, 70, 75)
DH 5   (62)
SE 5a   (63, 67, 77)
Bristol Fighter F 2b   (64, 72, 73)
Sopwith Camel   (65, 66, 68, 69, 71, 76, 79, 80)
Armstrong Whitworth FK 8   (74)

TYPES OF AIRCRAFT MACHINE GUNS
OF WORLD WAR I

ALLIED

Flexible Machine Guns

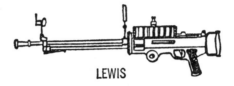

LEWIS

HOTCHKISS

Fixed Machine Guns

VICKERS

BROWNING

GERMAN

Flexible Machine Gun

PARABELLUM

Fixed Machine Gun

SPANDAU

TO THE MEMORY OF MANFRED VON RICHTHOFEN[1]

Reichsmarschall Hermann Göring

The heroes produced by the World War are countless. Throughout the world men used many weapons against each other in order to gain victory, and enormous results were achieved in the four years of battle. But no weapon of that wondrous and impressive age in which we lived was as striking to the imagination as that of the knightly battle we had to endure, the battle of the fliers who rose up from their fields to engage in the deadly combat of man against man. No one knew if he would come back as the victor or not at all. We Germans must be inspired and imbued with an indestructible pride that of all the champions to soar in combat above the earth, the highest success, the highest honor, the highest renown was won by a German. Manfred Freiherr von Richthofen became not only the greatest battle flyer of Germany, but of the world.

21 April 1933 marks the fifteenth anniversary of the day in which Rittmeister Freiherr von Richthofen, at the zenith of his glory, met a hero's death. I am grateful that this day shall be solemnly celebrated in the capital of the Reich and in his Silesian home of Schweidnitz. And I am glad that his heroic book, *Der Rote Kampfflieger,* in which he himself reports his deeds simply and modestly as he was, appears anew and shows the German nation the nature of the man who became and shall remain a

[1] This was the Foreword written by Hermann Göring for the publication of the second edition of Von Richthofen's memoirs, in 1933—the time of the Nazi takeover of power in Germany. It is bombastic, pompous, and boastful propaganda about German supremacy—all of which was obliterated by the smashing Allied victories of the First World War.

However, it is included here both for its historical association and because Göring was Von Richthofen's successor as commander of *Jagdgeschwader* 1 toward the end of the First World War, and was chief of the *Luftwaffe* in the Second World War.

symbol of the best virtues of the German people: bravery, gallantry, and love of fatherland.

Germany is awake. Germany must and will win back its world prominence. Without valor there is no state, there can be no proud and honorable nation. Manfred von Richthofen fought for Germany's greatness and power, training hundreds and hundreds of German men and youths, leading and preparing for battle, and finally giving up his own life. He knew at the time how decisive was superiority in the air in the fight for the victory of our people, and he surmised that surely its significance would increase in the future. Now we are engaged in a struggle for equal rights among the other nations of this earth. And it is the development of our air weapon that will be most hotly contested.

We will hold Manfred von Richthofen as a great symbol. His memory will help us to use all means in our power to reach our national goal of again giving Germany an air weapon equal to those of other nations, but superior to them in spirit and courageous sacrifice, as was the *Jagdgeschwader Richthofen* in the World War.

It was the highest honor for me as its last commander to be entrusted with the confidence of the leadership of the *Jagdgeschwader Richthofen*. That mission binds me to the future—I will carry this responsibility—in the spirit of Richthofen.

Hermann Göring
1933

CHRONOLOGICAL SUMMARY OF THE WAR— WESTERN FRONT AND OTHER SIGNIFICANT DATES

1914

June

28—Archduke Francis Ferdinand, heir to throne of Austria-Hungary, assassinated at Sarajevo, Bosnia.

July

18—Aviation Section of the U. S. Army's Signal Corps authorized by Congress.

28—Austria-Hungary declares war on Serbia.

29—Russia mobilizes.

August

1—Germany declares war on Russia.
France mobilizes.

2—Germany invades Luxembourg.

3—Germany declares war on France.

4—Germany invades Belgium. Halted at Liège.
Great Britain at war with Germany.

5—President Wilson tenders good offices of United States in interests of peace.

6—Austria-Hungary at war with Russia.

7—French invade Alsace. Marshal Joffre in supreme command of French army.
Montenegro at war with Austria. British Expeditionary Force lands at Ostend, Calais, and Dunkirk.

8—Serbia at war with Germany.
Portugal announces readiness to stand by alliance with England.

12—France and Great Britain at war with Austria-Hungary.
Montenegro at war with Germany.

13–15—British RFC Squadrons fly to France.

17—Belgian capital removed from Brussels to Antwerp. Liège captured by Germans.

19—Canadian Parliament authorizes raising expeditionary force. First RFC air reconnaissance patrol over the Western Front.

20—Germans occupy Brussels.

21—Battle of Charleroi.

22—RFC air reconnaissance patrol reports Von Kluck's enemy force advancing on British Front.

23—British at Battle of Mons.

24—Germans enter France near Lille.

25—Three RFC planes force down first German aircraft.

26—Louvain sacked and burned by Germans. Viviani, Premier of France.

28—Austria declares war on Belgium.

29—Russians invade Königsberg, East Prussia.

30—Amiens occupied by Germans.

31—Russian army in East Prussia defeated at Tannenberg by Germans under Von Hindenburg.

September

3—Paris in state of siege; government transferred to Bordeaux.

4—Germans occupy Rheims.

6–10—Battle of Marne. Von Kluck beaten by Marshal Joffre. German army retreats from Paris to Soissons-Rheims line.

14—French reoccupy Amiens and Rheims.

20—Rheims cathedral shelled by Germans.

22—First British raid on German Zeppelin sheds in Düsseldorf and Cologne.

24—Allies occupy Peronne.

28—German aircraft first use black cross insignia.

29—Antwerp bombardment begins.

October

2—British Admiralty announces intention to mine North Sea areas.

8—British naval aircraft destroy first Zeppelin in its shed at Düsseldorf.

9—Antwerp surrenders to Germans. Government removed to Ostend.

12—British aircraft on Western Front ordered to use national insignia.

13—British occupy Ypres.

14—Canadian Expeditionary Force of 32,000 men lands at Plymouth.

15—Germans occupy Ostend. Belgian Government removed to Havre, France.

21—Zeppelin sheds at Friedrichshafen bombed.

December

14—First Battle of Champagne.

16—German squadron bombards Hartlepool, Scarborough and Whitby on east coast of England.

25—British seaplanes raid Zeppelin sheds at Cuxhaven.

1915

January

Allied flier shoots down German plane with a rifle in the first aerial duel of the war.

First successful aerial photoreconnaissance.

Inception of artillery ranging and spotting from the air.

February

French Lieutenant Roland Garros downs enemy aircraft with fixed machine gun firing between propeller blades.

10—Russians defeated by Germans in Battle of Masurian Lakes.

18—German submarines begin "blockade" of British Isles.

19–20—First German Zeppelin raid on England.

March

Anthony Fokker perfects synchronized machine gun.

10—British take Neuve-Chapelle in Flanders.

15—First merchant ship attacked from the air.

April

22—Second Battle of Ypres. Poison gas first used by Germans in attack on Canadians.

26—First Victoria Cross awarded for an air action.

May

7—*Lusitania,* Cunard liner, sunk by German submarine off Kinsale Head, Irish coast, with loss of 1152 lives; 102 Americans.

23—Italy declares war on Austria-Hungary and begins invasion on a 60-mile front.

31—German Zeppelin bombs London for first time (LZ. 38).

June

4–6—German aircraft bombs English towns.

7—RNAS Flight Sublieutenant R. A. J. Warneford shoots down Zeppelin over Belgium (LZ. 37).

The LZ. 38 destroyed in its shed at Evere.

15—Allied aircraft bombs Karlsruhe, in retaliation for raids on England.

July

11—RNAS airplanes do artillery spotting in sinking of *Königsberg.*

31—Baden bombed by French aircraft.

August

12—First enemy ship torpedoed and sunk by British seaplane at the Dardanelles.

19—Colonel "Boom" Trenchard placed in command of the RFC in France.

September

25—Allies open Artois offensive and occupy Lens.

October

12—Edith Cavell, English nurse, shot by Germans for aiding British prisoners to escape from Belgium.

13—London bombed by Zeppelins; 55 persons killed; 114 injured.

14—Bulgaria at war with Serbia.

15—Great Britain declares war on Bulgaria.

17—France at war with Bulgaria.

19—Italy and Russia at war with Bulgaria.

29—Briand becomes Premier of France, succeeding Viviani.

November

17—Anglo-French war council hold first meeting in Paris.

December

15—General Sir Douglas Haig succeeded Field Marshal Sir John French as Commander-in-Chief of British forces in France.

1916

January

Introduction of formation flying.

29-31—German Zeppelins bomb Paris and towns in England.

February

10—British conscription law goes into effect.

21—Battle of Verdun begins. Germans take Haumont.

25—Fort Douaumont falls to Germans.

March

9—Germany declares war on Portugal on the latter's refusal to give up seized ships.

15—Austria-Hungary at war with Portugal.

21—*Escadrille Americaine,* N. 124, authorized by French Air Service. (Later known as *Lafayette Escadrille.*)

31—Melancourt taken by Germans in Battle of Verdun.

April

French arm Nieuport 11s with Le Prieur air-to-air rockets. Successfully down Zeppelin.

14—RNAS planes bomb Constantinople (Istanbul) and Adrianople.

19—President Wilson publicly warns Germany not to pursue submarine policies.

20—Russian troops landed at Marseilles for service on French Front.

Sergeant Eliott C. Cowdin, first American aviator awarded French *Médaille Militaire*.

May

15—Vimy Ridge gained by British.

22—French fighter pilots down 5 German observation balloons with **Le Prieur** rockets.

31—Battle of Jutland; British and German fleets engaged; heavy losses on both sides.

June

5—Kitchener, British Secretary of War, loses life when cruiser *Hampshire,* is sunk off the Orkney Islands.

6—Germans capture Fort Vaux in Verdun attack.

18—First American shot down, H. Clyde Balsley of the *Lafayette Escadrille.*

July

1—British and French attack north and south of the Somme.

RAF gains control of the air.

14—British cavalry penetrate German second line.

15—Longueval captured by British.

25—Pozieres occupied by British.

30—British and French advance between Delville Wood and the Somme.

British and French air services carry out combined operations for first time.

August

3—French recapture Fleury.

27—Rumania declares war on Austria-Hungary.

28—Italy at war with Germany.

28—Germany at war with Rumania.

31—Bulgaria at war with Rumania. Turkey at war with Rumania.

September

2–3—Lieutenant W. Leefe Robinson first to shoot down Zeppelin over England.

15—British capture Flers-Courcelette, and other German positions on Western Front, using "tanks" directed from the air.

26—Combles and Thiepval captured by British and French.

October

1—Zeppelin L. 31 shot down near London.

24—Fort Douaumont recaptured by French.

November

2—Fort Vaux evacuated by Germans.

7—Woodrow Wilson re-elected President of the United States.

13—British advance along the Ancre.

22—Emperor Franz Josef of Austria-Hungary dies. Succeeded by Charles I.

23—German warships bombard English coast.

28—First German daylight air raid on London.

December

7—David Lloyd George succeeds Asquith as Prime Minister of England.

12—Approval for RAF to expand to 106 regular squadrons and 95 reserve squadrons.

15—French complete recapture of ground taken by Germans in Battle of Verdun.

18—President Wilson makes peace overtures to belligerents.

26—Germany replies to President Wilson's note and suggests a peace conference.

30—French Government on behalf of Allies replies to President Wilson's note and refuses to discuss peace till Germany agrees to give "restitution, reparation and guarantees."

1917

January

22—President Wilson suggests to the belligerents a "peace without victory."

31—Germany announces unrestricted submarine warfare.

February

3—United States severs diplomatic relations with Germany.

Count Von Bernstorff is handed his passports.

17—British troops on the Ancre capture German positions.

28—United States makes public a communication from Germany to Mexico proposing an alliance, and offering as a reward the return of Mexico's lost territory in Texas, New Mexico, and Arizona (Zimmermann Telegram).

Submarine campaign of Germans results in the sinking of 134 vessels during February.

March

3—British advance on Bapaume.

4—Germans begin withdrawal along Hindenburg Line.

14—China breaks with Germany.

15—Czar Nicholas abdicates. Prince Lvoff heads new cabinet.

17—Bapaume falls to British. Roye and Lassigny occupied by French.

18—Peronne, Chaulnes, Nesle and Noyon evacuated by Germans, who retreat on an 85-mile front.

19—Alexander Ribot becomes French Premier, succeeding Briand.

26–31—British advance on Cambrai.

April

6—United States declares war on Germany.

7—Cuba and Panama at war with Germany.

8—Austria-Hungary breaks with United States.

9—Germans retreat before British on long front (Battle of Arras).

9—Bolivia breaks with Germany.

13—Vimy, Givenchy, Bailleul, and positions about Lens taken by Canadians.

20—Turkey breaks with United States.

30—Major William C. Mitchell, first American officer to fly over the enemy lines.

May

7—German bombers make first night raid on London.

9—Liberia breaks with Germany.

15—Marshal Pétain succeeds Marshal Nivelle as Commander-in-Chief of French armies.

16—Bullecourt captured by British in the Battle of Arras.

17—Honduras breaks with Germany.

18—Conscription bill signed by President Wilson.

19—Nicaragua breaks with Germany.

20—British seaplane sinks first submarine from the air.

24—France asks U. S. to furnish 5000 pilots, 50,000 mechanics, and 4500 planes by spring, 1918.

25—Twenty-one Gotha bombers make first mass daylight attack on England. 200 casualties.

26—Major T. F. Dodd appointed Aviation Officer on staff of Commander-in-Chief, American Expeditionary Forces (AEF).

June

2—U. S. Aviation Section redesignated Airplane Division, Signal Corps.

5—Registration day for new draft army in United States.

7—Messines-Wytschaete ridge in English hands.

8—General John J. Pershing, Commander-in-Chief of AEF, arrives in England en route to France.

13—588 casualties in first mass daylight raid on London by 14 Gothas.

18—Haiti breaks with Germany.

21—British War Office recommends expansion of RFC regular squadrons to 200.

30—Lieutenant Colonel Billy Mitchell replaces Major Dodd as Aviation Officer, AEF.

July

1—Russians begin offensive in Gallicia. Kerensky, Minister of War, leading in person.

3—AEF arrives in France.

4—First 8-cylinder Liberty engine, designed and built in 6 weeks, ready for testing.

6—Canadian House of Commons passes Compulsory Military Service Bill.

12—King Constantine of Greece abdicates in favor of his second son, Alexander.

16–23—Retreat of Russians on a front of 155 miles.

20—Drawing of draft numbers for American conscript army begins. Alexander Kerensky becomes Russian Premier, succeeding Lvoff.

22—Siam at war with Germany and Austria.

23—Major Benjamin D. Foulois appointed Officer-in-Charge, U. S. Airplane Division.

24—$640 million appropriated to expand U. S. Airplane Division to 9989 officers and 87,083 men.

27—British DH-4 arrives in U. S. to serve as production model.

August

2—Sopwith Pup successfully landed on deck of H.M.S. *Furious.*

7—Liberia at war with Germany.

8—Canadian Conscription Bill passes its third reading in Senate.

13—First Aero Squadron leaves England to join AEF in France.

14—China at war with Germany and Austria-Hungary.

15—St. Quentin Cathedral destroyed by Germans.

15—Canadian troops capture Hill 70, dominating Lens.

21—Zeppelin destroyed off Danish coast by aircraft from H.M.S. *Yarmouth.*

22—Last German daylight air raid on England in World War I.

September

3—Brigadier General William L. Kenly becomes first Chief of Air Service, AEF.

5—New American National Army begins to assemble.

11—Guynemer killed.

14—Paul Painlevé becomes French Premier, succeeding Ribot.

16—Russia proclaimed a republic by Kerensky.

20—Costa Rica breaks with Germany.

26—Zonnebeke, Polygon Wood and Tower Hamlets, east of Ypres, taken by British.

October

1—Launch aircraft from H.M.S. *Repulse.*

6—Peru and Uruguay break with Germany.

9—Poelcapelle and other German positions captured in Franco-British attack.

14—British form 41st Bomb Wing for strategic bombing of German industrial targets.

18—DH-4s ordered into mass production (4500 were built by the end of the war, of which 1213 reached the Front).

23—American troops in France fire their first shots in trench warfare. French advance northeast of Soissons.

26—Brazil at war with Germany.

29—First American-built DH-4 flight-tested at Dayton, Ohio.

November

1—Germans abandon position on Chemin des Dames.

3—Americans in trenches suffer 20 casualties in German attacks.

6—Passchendaele captured by Canadians.

7—The Russian Bolsheviks, led by Lenin and Trotsky, seize Petrograd and depose Kerensky.

9—Italians retreat to the Piave.

10—Lenin becomes Premier of Russia, succeeding Kerensky.

15—Georges Clemenceau becomes Premier of France, succeeding Painlevé.

20—Battle of Cambrai. Scout aircraft attack ground targets.

21—Ribecourt, Flesquieres, Havrincourt, Marcoing, and other German positions captured by the British.

23—Italians repulse Germans on the whole front from the Asiago Plateau to the Brenta River.

24—Battle of Cambrai. British tanks approach within 3 miles, capturing Bourlon Wood.

27—Brigadier General B. D. Foulois replaces Brigadier General William L. Kenly as Chief of Air Service, AEF.

December

1—German East Africa reported completely conquered.

Allies' Supreme War Council, representing the United States, France, Great Britain, and Italy, holds first meeting at Versailles.

3—Russian Bolsheviks arrange armistice with Germans.

5—British retire from Bourlon Wood, Graincourt and other positions west of Cambrai.

7—Finland declares independence.

8—Jerusalem, held by the Turks for 673 years, surrenders to British, under General Edmund Allenby.

8—Ecuador breaks with Germany.

10—Panama at war with Austria-Hungary.

11—United States at war with Austria-Hungary.

15—Armistice signed between Germany and Russia at Brest-Litovsk.

17—Coalition government of Sir Robert Borden is returned and conscription confirmed in Canada.

26—The Curtiss JN-4 ("Jenny") becomes basic trainer for American pilots.

1918

January

2—British Air Ministry formed.

3—Major General Sir Hugh Trenchard, first British Chief of Air Staff.

8—President Wilson proclaims his "Fourteen Points."

18—Major General Sir John Salmond succeeds Major General Sir Hugh "Boom" Trenchard as commander of the RFC in France.

19—American troops take over sector northwest of Toul.

20—Colonel Billy Mitchell, Chief of Air Service I Army Corps.

23—First AEF observation balloon ascends in France.

February

1—Argentine Minister of War recalls military attachés from Berlin and Vienna.

18—103rd Aero Squadron, AEF, made up of former members of the *Lafayette Escadrille,* begins operations at the Front.

22—American troops in Chemin des Dames sector.

26—First U. S. Air Service unit to serve with American troops at the Front was the 2nd Balloon Co.

March

1—Americans gain signal victory in salient north of Toul.

3—Peace treaty between Bolshevik government of Russia and the Central Powers signed at Brest-Litovsk.

4—Treaty signed between Germany and Finland.

5—Rumania signs preliminary treaty of peace with Central Powers.

7—First German bomber raid on London on a moonless night.

9—Russian capital moved from Petrograd to Moscow.

11—Lieutenant Paul Baer of the U. S. 103rd Aero Squadron awarded first Air Service Distinguished Service Cross.

14—Russo-German peace treaty ratified by All-Russian Congress of Soviets at Moscow.

Patrol by the U. S. 95th Aero Squadron constitutes first air action of the American 1st Pursuit Group.

19—Pilots of the 94th ("Hat-in-the-Ring") Squadron fly first operational flights across the lines.

20—U. S. 28th Aero Squadron attached by flights to RAF squadrons in France.

21—Germans begin great drive on 50-mile front from Arras to La Fère. Bombardment of Paris by German long-range gun from a distance of 76 miles.

24—Peronne, Ham and Chauny evacuated by Allies.

25—Bapaume and Nesle occupied by Germans.

29—Marshal Ferdinand Foch chosen Commander-in-Chief of all Allied Armies on the Western Front.

April

1—The RFC and RNAS combined to form the Royal Air Force (RAF).

American Aviation Headquarters opened in Rome.

9—Second German drive begun in Flanders.

10—First German drive halted before Amiens after maximum advance of 35 miles.

11—First U. S. patrol over enemy lines in World War I, made by 1st Observation Group in 2-seater Spads.

14—Lieutenant Douglas Campbell, 94th Aero Squadron, scores first victory of an American-trained pilot.

British Major General F. H. Sykes appointed Chief of Air Staff.

15—Second German drive halted before Ypres, after maximum advance of 10 miles.

21—Guatemala at war with Germany.

Baron Manfred von Richthofen, ranking German flier, killed.

23—British naval forces raid German submarine base in Zeebrugge, Belgium, and block channel. First U. S. shipment of Liberty engines arrives in France.

27—Sir William Weir becomes Secretary of State for the RAF.

29—Lieutenant Edward V. Rickenbacker shoots down his first German plane.

May

7—Nicaragua at war with Germany and her allies.

11—First American-built DH-4 powered by a Liberty engine delivered to the AEF. First flight in France made on May 17.

19—Major Raoul Lufbery, famous American aviator, killed.

19-20—Last German bomber raid on England in which casualties were inflicted.

20—Army Aviation separated from the Signal Corps.

24—Costa Rica at war with Germany and Austria-Hungary.

6 HS-1s, American Navy-built seaplanes, first to arrive in France.

27—Third German drive begins on Aisne-Marne Front of 30 miles between Soissons and Rheims.

28—Germans sweep on beyond the Chemin des Dames and cross the Vesle at Fismes. Cantigny taken by Americans in local attack.

29—Soissons evacuated by French.

Brigadier General Mason M. Patrick becomes new Chief of Air Service, AEF.

31—Marne River crossed by Germans, who reach Château-Thierry, 40 miles from Paris.

June

3-6—American Marines and soldiers check advance of Germans at Château-Thierry and Neuilly after maximum advance of Germans (32 miles). Beginning of American cooperation on major scale.

5—Major General Sir Hugh Trenchard commands British Independent Air Force for strategic bombing of Germany.

9-14—German drive on Western Front ended.

12—First day U. S day bombing by 96th Aero Squadron on railroad marshaling yards in France.

15-24—Austrian drive on Italian Front ends in complete failure.

30—American troops in France: 1,019,115.

July

1—Vaux taken by Americans.

3—Mohammed V, Sultan of Turkey, dies.

8—Sopwith Camels from the aircraft carrier *Furious* destroy Zeppelins L. 54 and L. 60.

10—Czechoslovaks, aided by Allies, take control of a long stretch of the Trans-Siberian Railway.

15—Haiti at war with Germany.

15—Defense of Château-Thierry blocks new German drive on Paris.

17—Lieutenant Quentin Roosevelt, youngest son of ex-President Theodore Roosevelt, killed in aerial battle near Château-Thierry.

18—French and Americans begin counteroffensive on Marne-Aisne Front.

20—U. S. 148th Aero Squadron begins operation with the RAF near Dunkirk.

23—French take Oulchy-le-Château and drive the Germans back 10 miles between the Aisne and the Marne.

30—Allies astride the Ourcq; Germans in full retreat to the Vesle.

August

1—Sergeant Joyce Kilmer, American poet and critic, aged 31, dies in battle with the U. S. "Fighting 69th" Regiment.

2—French troops recapture Soissons.

18 U. S.-built DH-4s with Liberty engines, fly their first patrol along the Front.

3—President Wilson announces new policy regarding Russia and agrees to cooperate with Great Britain, France and Japan in sending forces to Murmansk, Archangel and Vladivostok.

3—Allies sweep on between Soissons and Rheims, driving the enemy from his base at Fismes and capturing the entire Aisne-Vesle Front.

5—Last Zeppelin raid on England. L. 70 shot down.

7—Franco-American troops cross the Vesle.

8—New Allied drive begun by British Field Marshal Haig in Picardy, penetrating enemy Front 14 miles.

10—Montdidier recaptured.

11—Sopwith Camel launched from towed lighter shoots down Zeppelin L. 53.

13—Lassigny *massif* taken by French.

15—Canadians capture Damery and Parvillers, northwest of Roye.

21—Battle of Bapaume.

26—Battle of the Scarpe.

28—Battle of the Somme (1918).

29—Noyon and Bapaume fall in new Allied advance.

September

1—Australians take Peronne.

Americans fight for the first time on Belgian soil and capture Voormezeele.

11—Germans are driven back to the Hindenburg Line, which they held in November 1917.

12—Registration day for new U. S. draft of men between 18 and 45.

Lieutenant Frank Luke, the American "Balloon Buster" of the 27th Aero Squadron, scores his first victory.

13—Americans begin vigorous offensive in St. Mihiel Sector on 40-mile front. 1481 Allied planes under command of Brigadier General Billy Mitchell, largest air armada ever assembled, participates in the offensive.

14—St. Mihiel recaptured from Germans. General Pershing announces entire St. Mihiel salient erased, liberating more than 150 square miles of French territory which had been in German hands since 1914.

19–20—RFC destroys Turkish Seventh Army in Palestine, from the air.

25—British take 40,000 prisoners in Palestine offensive.

Lieutenant E. V. Rickenbacker attacks 7 enemy planes. He later received the Medal of Honor for this exploit.

27—Franco-Americans in drive from Rheims to Verdun take 30,-000 prisoners.

Begin attack on Hindenburg Line.

28—Belgians attack enemy from Ypres to North Sea, gaining 4 miles.

29—Bulgaria surrenders to General Franchet d'Esperey, the Allied commander.

30—British-Belgian advance reaches Roulers.

October

1—St. Quentin, cornerstone of Hindenburg Line, captured.

Allies bomb Germans, using electrical bomb release for first time.

Damascus occupied by British in Palestine campaign.

2—Lens evacuated by Germans. The United States "Bug," a guided missile, successfully flight-tested at Dayton, Ohio.

3—Albania cleared of Austrians by Italians.

4—King Ferdinand of Bulgaria abdicates; Boris succeeds.

5—Prince Maximilian, new German Chancellor, pleads with President Wilson to ask Allies for armistice.

7—Berry-au-Bac taken by French.

9—Cambrai in Allied hands.

11—Americans advance through Argonne Forest.

12—German Foreign Secretary, Solf, says plea for armistice is made in name of German people; agrees to evacuate all foreign soil.

American pursuit pilots participate in first U. S. night airfighter action.

13—Laon and La Fère abandoned by Germans.

Grandpré captured by Americans after 4-day battle.

14—President Wilson refers Germans to Marshal Foch for armistice terms.

A British Handley-Page drops a 1650-lb. bomb, largest of the war.

16—Lille entered by British patrols.

17—Ostend, German submarine base, taken by land and sea forces.

Douai falls to Allies.

19—Bruges and Zeebrugge taken by Belgian and British forces.

25—Beginning of terrific Italian drive, which nets 50,000 prisoners in five days.

26—"Boom" Trenchard appointed Commander-in-Chief, Inter-Allied Independent Air Force.

31—Turkey surrenders; armistice takes effect at noon; conditions include free passage through Dardanelles.

November

1—Cléry-le-Grand captured by American First Army troops.

3—Americans sweep ahead on 50-mile front above Verdun; enemy in full retreat. German fleet mutinies at Kiel.

Official reports announce capture of 362,350 Germans since July 15. Austria surrenders, signing armistice with Italy at 3 P.M. after 500,000 prisoners have been taken.

4—Americans advance beyond Stenay and strike at Sedan.

Victory of Vittorio Veneto.

7—American "Rainbow" Division and parts of 1st Division enter suburbs of Sedan.

8—Heights south of Sedan seized by Americans.

9—Maubeuge captured by Allies.

10—Canadians take Mons in irresistible advance.

The 3rd Pursuit Group flies last American patrol over enemy lines.

11—Germany surrenders; armistice takes effect at 11 A.M. American flag hoisted on Sedan Front.

SPECIFICATIONS AND DATA ON AIRCRAFT
FLOWN OR FOUGHT BY VON RICHTHOFEN

GERMAN AIRCRAFT

Albatros C III

Two-seater reconnaissance and bomber machine (1916–18). Von Richthofen, Udet and Göring began their flying careers in the Albatros C III. The C III was succeeded by the C V.

Engine—170-hp Mercedes
Wingspan—38 ft. 6 ins.
Weight—3044 lbs. loaded
Length—27 ft. 6 ins.
Speed—87.5 mph at sea level
Ceiling—12,000 ft.
Endurance—4 hrs. 30 mins.
Armament—1 fixed Spandau machine gun in front and 1 flexible Parabellum in the rear

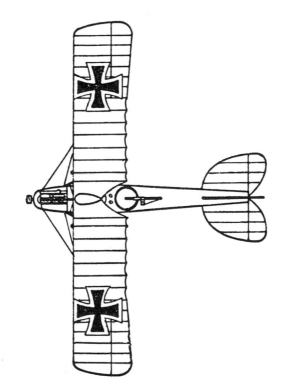

Albatros D II

Single-seater scout. Its predecessor, Albatros D I, entered the fray in August 1916 as a replacement for the Fokker *Eindekker*, which could not cope with the British DH 2 and French Nieuport 11. The D II model had improved visibility and, together with the D I and the Halberstadt scouts, proved more than a match for the Allied aircraft. The Baron flew an all-red Albatros D II.

Engine—160-hp Mercedes, 160-hp Benz
Wingspan—27 ft. 11 ins.
Weight—1967 lbs. loaded
Length—24 ft.
Speed—109 mph maximum
Ceiling—17,000 ft.
Endurance—1 hr. 30 mins.
Armament—2 fixed Spandau machine guns

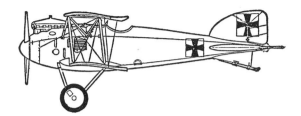

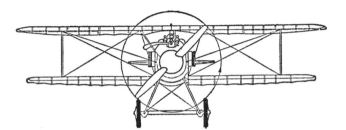

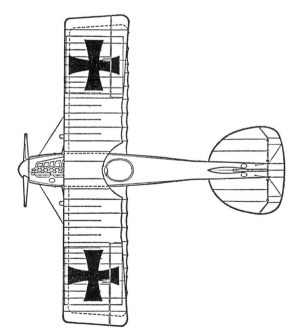

Albatros D V

Single-seater scout of early 1917, one of the most successful of its line. It replaced the earlier excellent D I and D II of 1916. The D III was itself replaced later in 1917 by the D V, which resembled it closely in physical appearance.

Engine—175-hp Mercedes
Wingspan—29 ft. 7 ins.
Weight—2050 lbs. loaded
Length—24 ft. 2 ins.
Speed—120 mph at sea level
Ceiling—18,000 ft.
Endurance—2 hrs.
Armament—2 fixed Spandau machine guns

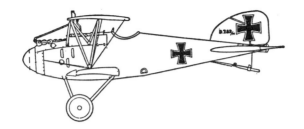

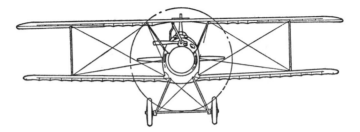

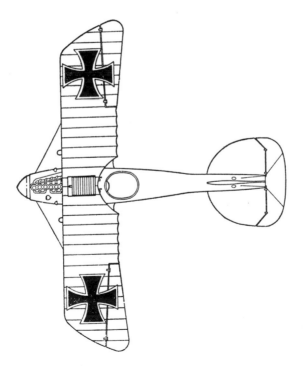

Fokker *Eindekker* E III

Single-seater scout or fighter, appeared at the front in December 1915. Its predecessor, Model E I, was the first to have a fixed machine gun synchronized to fire between the propeller blades. It was flown with great success by Boelcke and Immelmann.

Engine—130 Oberursel rotary
Wingspan—37 ft. 9 ins.
Length—23 ft. 6½ ins.
Weight—1340 lbs. loaded
Speed—95 mph
Ceiling—12,000 ft.
Endurance—1 hr. 30 mins.
Armament—1 fixed Spandau machine gun

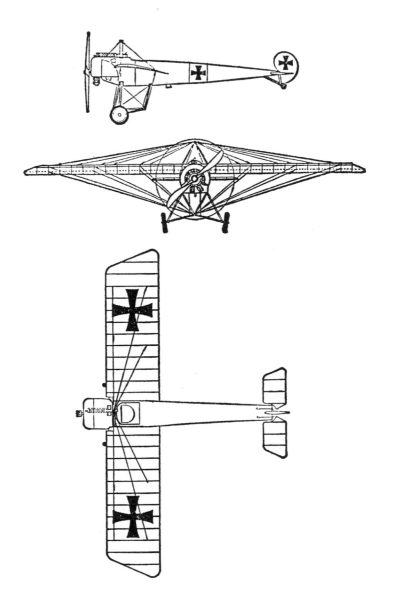

Fokker D VII

Single-seater scout (1918), acclaimed as the best fighter plane developed in the war. It was specifically mentioned in the Treaty of Versailles.

Engine—160-, 180-, 200-, or 220-hp Mercedes, 185-hp B.M.W.
Wingspan—29 ft. 3½ ins.
Length—23 ft.
Weight—1960 lbs. loaded
Speed—135 mph (220 hp)
Ceiling—22,000 ft. (185 hp)
Endurance—1 hr. 45 mins.
Armament—2 fixed Spandau machine guns

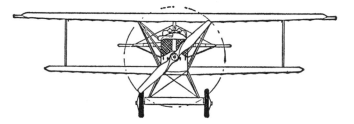

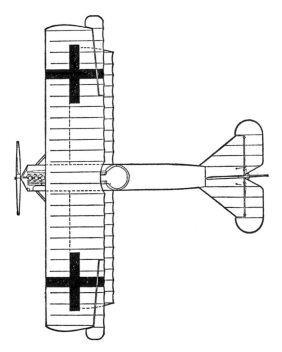

Fokker Dr I Triplane

Single-seater scout, arrived on the Western Front in August 1917. It was the all-red aircraft flown by Von Richthofen in his last fight against Roy Brown's flight of Sopwith Camels.

Engine—110-hp Oberursel rotary
Wingspan—23 ft. 7 ins.
Weight—1289 lbs. gross
Length—19 ft.
Speed—122 mph at 8900 ft.
Ceiling—20,000 ft.
Endurance—2 hrs. 30 mins.
Armament—2 fixed Spandau machine guns

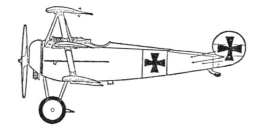

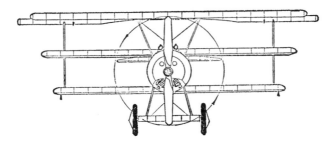

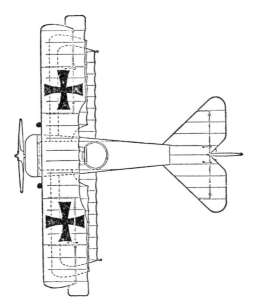

Halberstadt D II

Single-seater fighter (1916), used by the Red Baron during January 1917 when his Albatros was damaged. The Halberstadt, together with the Albatros scouts, succeeded the Fokker *Eindekker* and bested the DH 2 and Nieuport 11.

Engine—120-hp Argus, 120-hp Mercedes
Wingspan—28 ft. 10 ins.
Weight—1606 lbs. loaded
Length—23 ft. 11 ins.
Speed—90 mph at sea level
Ceiling—13,000 ft.
Endurance—1 hr. 30 mins.
Armament—1 or 2 fixed Spandau or Maxim machine guns

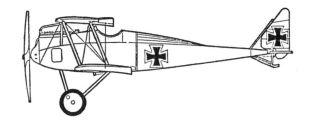

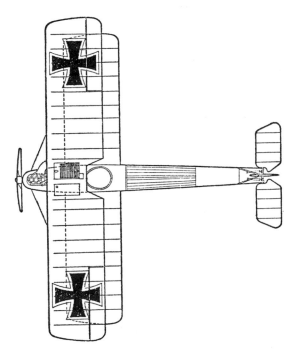

Pfalz D III

Single-seater scout (1917). The Pfalz and the Albatros fighters were very similar in appearance and, in fact, were grouped together within the same squadrons. Some of the *staffeln* that made up the Baron's *Jagdgeschwader* 1 were equipped with the Pfalz D III.

Engine—160-hp Mercedes
Wingspan—30 ft. 11 ins.
Weight—2056 lbs. loaded
Length—23 ft. 2 ins.
Speed—103 mph
Ceiling—17,580 ft.
Endurance—2 hrs. 30 mins.
Armament—2 fixed Spandau machine guns

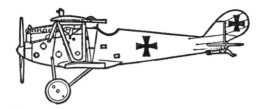

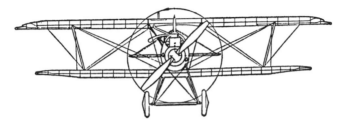

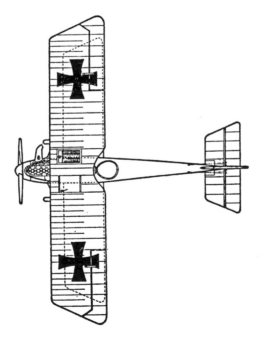

ALLIED AIRCRAFT

BE 2c

Two-seater reconnaissance aircraft (prewar). It was one of the poorer products of the British Royal Aircraft Factory at Farnborough. Except for the twin skids between the wheels, to prevent "nose-over" crashes, the 2c closely resembled its successor 2d, 2e and 12b models.

Engine—RAF la, 90–100 hp
Wingspan—37 ft.
Length—27 ft. 3 ins.
Weight—2142 lbs. loaded
Speed—72 mph at 6500 ft.
Ceiling—11,000 ft.
Endurance—3 hrs. 15 mins.
Armament—1 or 2 flexible Lewis guns

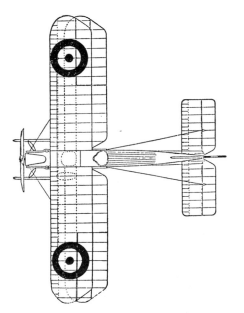

Bristol Fighter F 2b

Two-seater fighter and reconnaissance aircraft (1916). The "Brisfit" was one of the better airplanes developed during the war. Four of a flight of six Bristol F 2a's went down before the onslaught of Von Richthofen's *staffel* at the Battle of Arras, and the Bristol Fighter was considered a "jinx." A later change of tactics, however, made it a most formidable fighter.

Engine—200-hp Sunbeam Arab, 200-hp Hispano-Suiza
Wingspan—39 ft. 3 ins.
Weight—2630 lbs. loaded
Length—24 ft. 9 ins.
Speed—120 mph at sea level
Ceiling—20,000 ft.
Endurance—3 hrs.
Armament—1 fixed Vickers (pilot's) and 1 or 2 flexible Lewis guns on Scarff mount in rear (observer's)

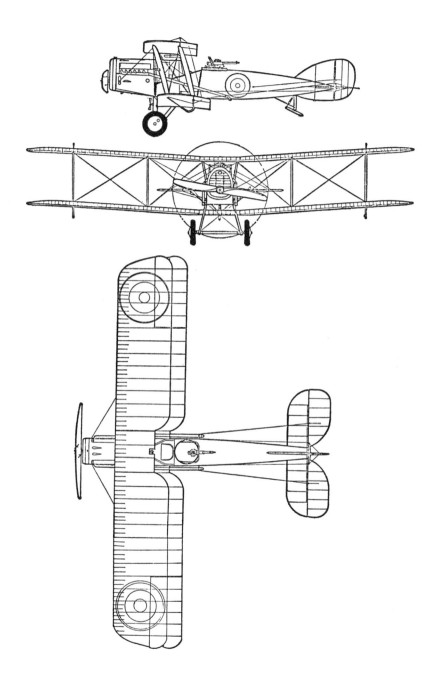

DH 2

Single-seater scout (1916). This pusher-type aircraft made up Britain's first all-fighter squadron—No. 24, under the command of Major Lanoe G. Hawker. Von Richthofen is credited with shooting Hawker down.

Engine—100-hp Gnôme Monosoupape
Wingspan—28 ft. 3 ins.
Weight—1320 lbs. loaded
Length—25 ft. 3 ins.
Speed—93 mph at sea level
Ceiling—1400 ft.
Endurance—2 hrs. 45 mins.
Armament—1 flexible Lewis gun

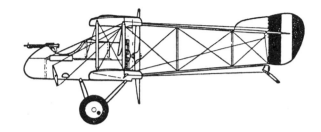

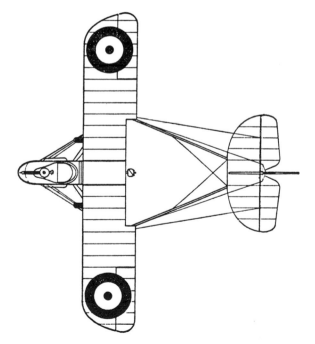

FE 2b

Two-seater fighter reconnaissance aircraft manufactured by the Royal Aircraft Factory (1916). Before the Allies had a synchronized machine gun, this pusher-type plane (with the engine mounted behind the pilot) left the observer, in the forward cockpit, free to fire without interference from the propeller. The FE 2d, with a larger engine, resembled it very closely.

Engine—120- or 160-hp Beardmore
Wingspan—47 ft. 10 ins.
Weight—3037 lbs. loaded
Length—32 ft. 3 ins.
Speed—81 mph at 6500 ft.
Ceiling—11,000 ft.
Endurance—3 hrs.
Armament—1 or 2 flexible Lewis guns forward (observer's) and
    1 or 2 flexible Lewis guns in the rear (pilot's)

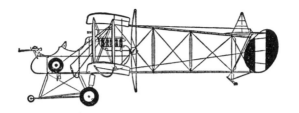

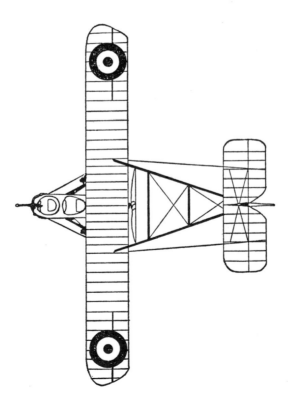

Nieuport 17

Single-seater scout (1916–17). A trim little aircraft, successor to the Nieuport 11. It was the favorite of many Allied aces.

Engine—110-hp Le Rhône rotary.
Wingspan—27 ft.
Length—19 ft. 6 ins.
Weight—1233 lbs. loaded.
Speed—107 mph at 6500 ft.
Ceiling—17,400 ft.
Endurance—2 hrs.
Armament—1 Lewis gun mounted on upper wing, fired over propeller and could be raised or lowered but not swung from side to side, or 1 fixed synchronized Vickers gun on fuselage forward of pilot.

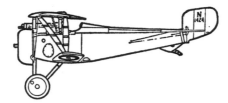

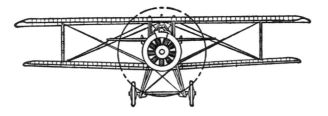

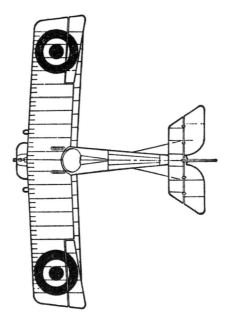

RE 8

Two-seater reconnaissance aircraft (1916). The RE 8 (Reconnaissance Experimental No. 8) was a product of the British Royal Aircraft Factory at Farnborough. It was superseded by the infinitely superior Bristol Fighter.

Engine—150-hp RAF 4a
Wingspan—42 ft. 7 ins.
Weight—2678 lbs. loaded
Length—27 ft. 10 ins.
Speed—102 mph at 6500 ft.
Ceiling—13,000 ft.
Endurance—4 hrs. 30 mins.
Armament—1 fixed Vickers on left side of fuselage (pilot's) and 1 or 2 flexible Lewis guns on Scarff mounting in rear cockpit (observer's)

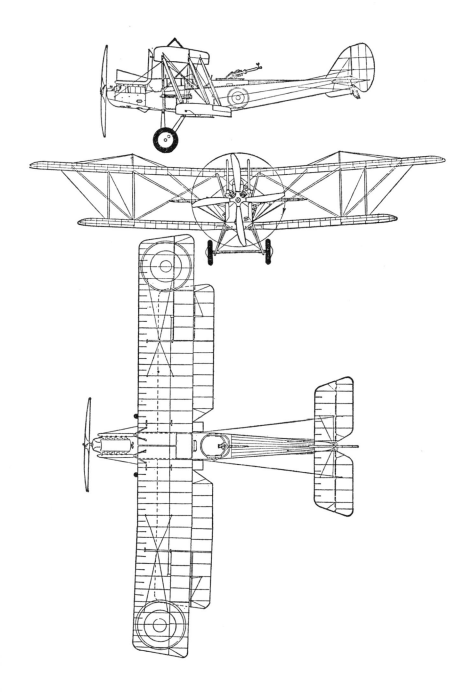

SE 5a

Single-seater scout (1917–18). This was an improvement over the SE 5, both being products of the Royal Aircraft Factory at Farnborough. RFC aces Bishop, Mannock and McCudden scored most of their victories in this type aircraft.

Engine—200-, 220-, or 240-hp Hispano-Suiza, 200-hp Wolseley Viper
Wingspan—26 ft. 7½ ins.
Weight—2048 lbs. loaded
Length—20 ft. 11 ins.
Speed—132 mph at 6500 ft.
Ceiling—20,000 ft.
Endurance—2 hrs. 30 mins.
Armament—1 fixed Vickers gun, and 1 Lewis gun mounted on upper wing, fired over propeller and could be raised or lowered but not swung from side to side

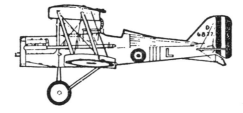

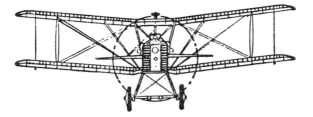

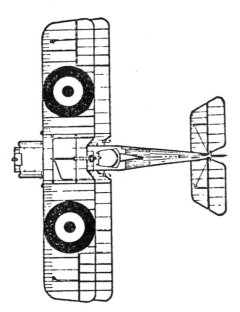

Sopwith 1½ Strutter

Two-seater fighter, reconnaissance and bomber aircraft (1915). The 1½ Strutter was the first British aircraft to enter combat with a synchronized Vickers machine gun. The U. S. Air Service purchased 514 of this model.

Engine—110- or 130-hp Clerget rotary
Wingspan—33 ft. 6 ins.
Weight—1259 lbs. empty
Length—25 ft. 3 ins.
Speed—100 mph
Ceiling—15,500 ft.
Endurance—3 hrs. 45 mins.
Armament—1 fixed Vickers machine gun forward, and 1 flexible Lewis machine gun in the rear cockpit (observer's)

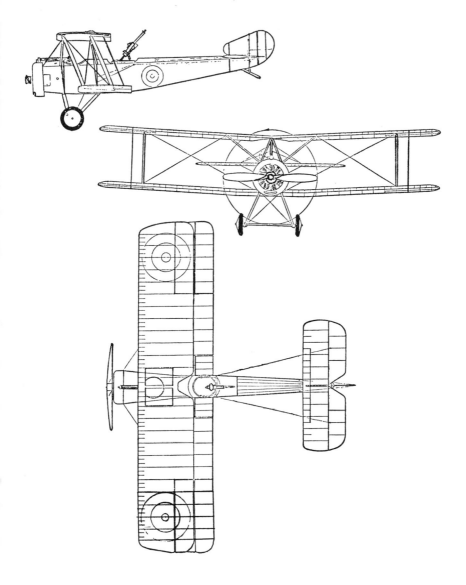

Sopwith Pup

Single-seater scout (1916), direct predecessor of the great Sopwith Camel. Two "Pups" fell before the Red Baron's guns—his sixteenth and sixty-first victories.

Engine—80-hp Le Rhône, 100-hp Gnôme Monosoupape
Wingspan—26 ft. 9 ins.
Weight—1225 lbs. loaded (80 hp), 1313 lbs. loaded (100 hp)
Length—19 ft. 7 ins.
Speed—106.5 mph at 6500 ft. (80 hp)
Ceiling—17,500 ft. (80 hp)
Endurance—3 hrs.
Armament—1 fixed synchronized Vickers. McCudden had a Lewis gun, instead of the Vickers gun, mounted on the top wing of his Pup.

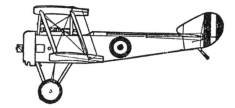

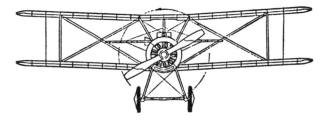

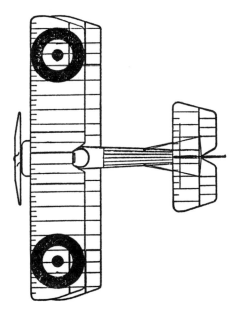

Sopwith Camel F 1

Single-seater scout (1917–18). More enemy aircraft were destroyed by this British fighter than by any other in the First World War. It was flown by Canadian Captain Roy Brown in the action in which Von Richthofen was shot down on 21 April 1918.

Engine—110-hp Le Rhône rotary, 130-hp Clerget rotary
Wingspan—28 ft.
Weight—1453 lbs. loaded
Length—18 ft. 8 ins.
Speed—119 mph (Le Rhône), 113 mph (Clerget)
Ceiling—24,000 ft. (Le Rhône), 19,000 ft. (Clerget)
Endurance—2 hrs. 45 mins. (Le Rhône), 2 hrs. 30 mins. (Clerget)
Armament—2 fixed Vickers machine guns

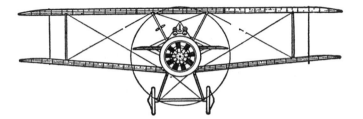

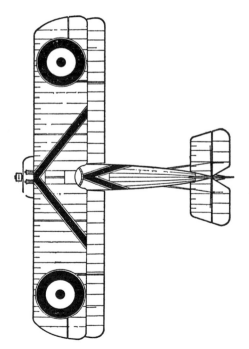

Spad VII

Single-seater scout (1916). This French-designed fighting plane was also used by the RFC and Americans in the *Lafayette Escadrille*. It was preferred by many over the later Spad XIII.

Engine—150-hp Hispano-Suiza
Wingspan—25 ft. 8 ins.
Weight—1632 lbs. loaded
Length—20 ft. 3 ins.
Speed—120 mph
Ceiling—17,500 ft.
Endurance—2 hrs. 30 mins.
Armament—1 fixed Vickers machine gun

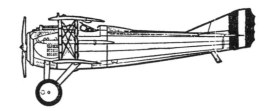

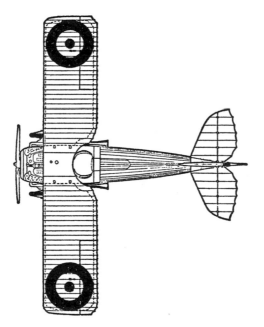